# FOUR PAWED ANGELS
## By K.G. Keough-Huff

I am a dog person. I walk around my house and there are dog pictures, paintings, all kinds of presents from family and friends. I even have a dog lamp that was made for me by my niece, Grace. When I get birthday cards they often have a picture or dog theme. Dogs have enriched my life.

This book is written in memory of my Soul Dog, Gypsy. My dogs have taught me so much about unconditional love. Whenever I was upset my dogs, especially Gypsy, always tried to do something to help me. They showed their concern for me by nudging me, putting their head on my lap, and kissing my tears. Through them, I have learned to live in my heart, by focusing on kindness and the good I can do for others.

As you read the chapters in this book you will see the many emotions and connections that dogs and humans share. Enjoy! – K.G. Keough-Huff

# Table of Contents - Four Pawed Angels

**Page**

| | |
|---|---|
| 5 | **Introduction** |
| 13 | **PART 1: My Angels – Tammy, Frosty, Disney, Gypsy, Brittany, Nicky, Petey** |
| 46 | **PART 2: 4 Pawed Angel Tales** |
| 48 | **Abuse, Neglect and Forced to Endure** |
| | Abuse/Anxiety/Stress/Fear |
| | Sadness/Grieving/Depression |
| | Crying/Passive Aggressive/Anger |
| | Pain & Shock |
| 84 | **Making the Connection from Healing to Forgiveness – Who Rescues Who?** |
| | Trust-Faith/Unconditional Love |
| | Show Dogs /Rescue Me |
| 102 | **Growing into Loyalty and Protection** |
| | Generosity /Loyalty - Protection |
| | Resilience |
| 117 | **Coming into Fullness of Life – Joy and Silliness** |
| | Telepathy – Dognition - Visualization |
| | Funny Stuff & EEEWW—GROSS! |

       Spontaneity - Curiosity
**134**  **Aging and Saying Goodbye**
       Doggy Dementia/Dignity
       Having Accidents
       Saying Goodbye
**153**  **Dreams**

**156**  **Acknowledgements**
**157**  **Dedication**
**158**  **Recommended Websites & Readings**

## Introduction

This book is about celebrating the lives of those who have been rescued and the rescuers who saved them. Over the course of my life I have been rescued by, and have rescued, both dogs and people. In my case I would first have to ask, "Who rescued who?" My dogs have saved me and done as much for me as I have for them. From them I have learned how to survive abuse and neglect. From my dogs I have learned to heal and forgive. They have taught me the blessing of loyalty and protection. They have helped bring me into the fullness of my life by adding joy and silliness to my days. And finally they have taught me grace and dignity in aging and saying goodbye.

My love affair with dogs began when I was little and my parents got a collie that looked exactly like Lassie, a television show we watched back in the 1960's where Lassie was the star. The show centered around Lassie, with a continuous theme of the dog watching over her human family and solving all sorts of problems.

Our dog was named Tammy, and she was the star of our house. She was a herding dog who watched out for us. In most of my childhood memories she was there, not always participating but on the outskirts, watching. Tammy seemed so much more mature, so much more aware than our perception of what a dog knows. When I looked into her eyes, she would look into mine, past them into my soul, with a wisdom that was startling. I felt a closeness to her, a spiritual connection. When those moments happened I was filled with joy. Tammy's joy reflected back to me, with her looking so intently with a smile and eyes so bright and happy.

Recently, I was talking to my brother-in-law Ray about this book and a talk I was going to give at my church. When I told him the title of my talk, "Finding God in Dog," he said "Well, that should be easy, just tell them to look in the mirror! God is Dog spelled backwards!"

There is joy in finding God in Dog. My sister Pam has 2 dogs, Maggie and Rufus, and a cat, Mr. Snibbets. Maggie is a Australian cattle dog and Rufus is a Mexican terrier mix. Mr. Snibbets is all white with green eyes but is really a dog born in a cat's body. I love going there since I can count on great joy and affection each time I visit. I arrive and quietly enter the house. All is still until I say "Where are my Precious Poopsies? " Then the greetings begin. They come flying into the kitchen from wherever they were and the next 5 minutes are spent getting kisses, giving pats and hugs. Hair is flying (not mine), tails are wagging, Mr. Snibbets rubs up against my leg. They are so happy to see me! I think that when some people find God they experience that same joy, that unconditional love. We don't wag our tails but there is a similar joy in knowing that there is a God, or Higher Power.

Maggie and Rufus

Recent research indicates that people who have dogs generally live 10 years longer than those who don't. Those who show dogs are likely to live 20 years longer. Dogs provide many wellness benefits. People with dogs sleep better, weigh less and get more exercise than those who don't have dogs. There are also studies being done on dogs and aging. Why? They share the same environment, often eat the same food, they sleep in our homes, even in our own beds. Dogs get sick with the same illnesses we get. They get arthritis and heart disease, and many of the same cancers we deal with.

Dog people or "doggie devotee's" will do anything for their dogs. The loving bond is so strong. Recently my sister Pam's dog, Maggie, became very ill. Pam took Maggie to the vet to see what could be done to help her, but was cautious about spending too much money on a dog...until she learned that Maggie's condition might be fatal. Cost concerns went right out the window. Pam said, "I didn't even care about the cost. I just wanted her to get better. My husband Ray, who repairs and sells Mopeds, told me he would start a "Mopeds for Maggie" campaign to raise money to pay for the cost of treatment. Maggie came home a few days later and is doing well." Yes, we will do anything for our dogs.

Maggie

Dogs, like us, start to slow down when they age. Things don't work as well. We don't run as fast, see as well, our hearing starts to diminish and we can even have 'accidents'. What I have learned from my aging dogs is patience and acceptance. They can't help what is happening to them, just like we can't. So I have learned to accept what happens to me, like when my shoulder hurts and I have no idea why, or I can't find my phone and have my wife, Chris, call it so I can locate it, or I walk around looking for something and can't remember what I am looking for. I try not to be angry or frustrated with myself.

Our aging dogs can teach us a lot. Today when I look in Petey's eyes, my now 16 year old, with his cataracts, the 2 teeth he has left, his sudden 'walk about's' (I have no idea where he is going, neither does he), his accidents, his 5:00 a.m. good morning kisses, I thank God for bringing Petey into my life and for every second we have and for every one we have left. When I look in Petey's eyes, I see God in dog smiling back at me.

Dogs provide us with so much love. I think all dogs are therapy dogs in some way. Therapy dogs that are trained do provide the missing link that a disabled person needs. They help people who have seizure disorders and can do almost anything to support a person with disabilities. Aren't we all disabled in some way? Somehow dogs bridge a gap or fill a need that brings us to a greater fullness of life.

Over the course of writing <u>Four Pawed Angels</u> I had the opportunity to interview many people from all walks of life who owned or worked with dogs. Without exception, each interview brought tears and laughter as people recalled stories about their dogs. Thank you to all of my contributors for sharing their experiences.

My Angels – Tammy Keough, Frosty Keough, Disney Keough-Huff, Gypsy Keough-Huff, Brittany Keough-Huff, Nicky Keough-Huff, and Petey Keough-Huff

Dorsie Kovacs and Sharon Johnson and their angels Gus, Critter, Roxanne, and Crackers

Pam, Ray, Mark, and Samantha Doucette and their angels Molly, Maggie, Rufus, and Mr. Snibbets.

Christine Gerhardt and her angels Cassie and Cletis

Grace Gerhardt for the dog lamp and John Gerhardt for his pictures and gift, and their understanding of how much my dogs meant to me.

Rita Schiano and her angels Jazzy, Frisco, Satche, and Jessie

Susan Rodgers and her angels Gillis and Geordie, and many more.

Diane Mossa and her angels Bailey, Bandit, and Zeus

Heidi Knowlton and Raja Mukerjee and their angels Pasha, Glob, and Sassy

Pam Alvarez and the many dogs she has rescued through Abby's Little Friends

Cindy and Jim Craig and their dog Muppet

Pam and Pat Patterson and their angels Snickers, Bailey, Doc, Bubba, Angel, and many more.

# PART I:
# MY ANGELS

Dog Lamp by Grace Gerhardt

**TAMMY**

Tammy came to our house when I was four years old. She was a collie and looked exactly like the dog on "Lassie", a popular television show in the 1960's. I remember her 'herding' us children, nipping at our ankles lightly enough so that it tickled and made us laugh. She was great with kids and adults, and other dogs too.

Tammy was a very nurturing dog, with a 'mother hen' mentality. It seemed that she felt her role was to guard and play with her human 'children'. I can remember her sitting under my baby sister Pam's bassinet where she slept after Pam was born…….not growling or anything but just sitting with her head on her paws, watching everyone who came into the room. If our mother came in to pick up the baby, Tammy would follow, keeping the baby near her.

Tammy used to play her own version of 'Hide and Seek' with us. We would run around the house and she would take off in the opposite direction and 'surprise' us. We would squeal with laughter, turn around and head off. Tammy would then dash off back around the house and surprise us again!

Poor Tammy was often blamed for anything that we children did wrong. I remember one time I snuck some chocolate cookies from the cookie jar after being told by my mother not to take them. A couple of hours later she confronted me and asked "Who took cookies from the cookie jar? I pointed at the dog and said "Tammy did it." Mom paused, smiled and said, "That Tammy is an amazing dog!" Of course our parents knew that Tammy was not responsible for anything other than being a very loving animal.

One of my favorite memories of her is when she would lie in front of the fireplace. With the fire roaring, she would try to get as close as possible.  We would try to nudge her out of the way but she wouldn't budge.

We were all very sad as Tammy aged. Her older days were difficult not being able to get up, and having accidents, which she was so ashamed of.  Yet we loved her so and kept her as long as we could.  When my father took Tammy to be 'put down', it was one of the only times I ever saw him cry.

Having Tammy as my childhood dog and the wonderful experiences we had with her made getting a dog as an adult a natural addition to my family.  All of my siblings ended up with dogs, and some have cats too. However, Tammy will always hold a special place in our hearts.

**FROSTY**

After a few years without a dog, my mother brought home "Frosty", an Irish Wolfhound/German Shepherd mix. He was a few years old and had been left at Buddy Dog, a local dog shelter, when his owners had to move and could not bring him. He was the sweetest dog, but he was huge, weighing in at over 100 pounds. When my father saw him he said to my mother, "I thought you were looking for a little 'lap dog'. "He looked much smaller in the crate", was my mother's reply.

Frosty was with our family for 8 years and there are many stories about his unique personality! I remember one day my younger sister, Christine, planned to go Roller Skating in the street and had decided to bring Frosty along. I was looking out the bay window in the family room when I was surprised to see Frosty running down the street with my sister holding onto his leash for dear life as he pulled her along. Her pigtails were flying back, her knees bent to keep her balance on her roller skates. I'll never forget that they both were smiling as they raced down the street.

Another Frosty story I remember was when I was staying at my parent's house, having broken my leg and needing extra help from family while I recovered. I had gone with another one of my sister's, Valerie, to get McDonald's for dinner for the entire family. We came back with several bags of food and I helped by carrying a couple of bags with my crutches. My sister went ahead of me and opened the front door. I looked up to see Frosty bounding out of the house making a beeline for me. Despite my yelling "No! No! No!" Frosty was so happy to see me, he knocked me over by standing on his two back legs and putting his paws on my shoulders. The bags went flying everywhere and I think Frosty got a hamburger or two and some fries before I was able to get up and salvage what was left.

There were times when Frosty wanted to be really small and quiet, like when he was interested in sleeping on the bed. He had a habit of coming onto my bed in the middle of the night when I was asleep. He would slowly take over during the night and I would wake up at the edge with Frosty's paws on my back, gently pushing me off the bed!

My sister Pam recalls how the family cat, Schnappsy, would chase Frosty around the yard. "It was hysterical watching our small cat chasing this huge 110 pound dog! He was the most gentle dog we ever had."

Frosty also loved car rides and he filled the back of our Volkswagon rabbit, sticking his head out the window, which was quite a sight. Pam says, "We would take Frosty to the Firefighting Academy where my mother worked and he would walk right into the building."

We were all saddened when Frosty died at the age of 10. Frosty died in the late afternoon with most of the family providing comfort. He will always be remembered as a wonderful, sweet dog.

**GYPSY**

If you are lucky, you will find that person in your life who becomes your Soul Mate. And some of us find our Soul Dog too. Gypsy was my Soul Dog. Of all my dog angels, the ones that took care of me over the years, he was the one who connected to my soul and spirit. We were alike. He was a little wild, adventurous, spontaneous, didn't always listen, got lost, came home, very loyal, and full of energy. Just like me.

    Gypsy was a 7 month old stray, an Australian shepherd/Husky mix, when he followed me onto the campus at Milton Academy where I worked, and eventually to my apartment on campus. It was September 1, 1993 when Gypsy arrived at our doorstep, looking lost, thirsty, and hungry. We did not have a dog yet but were purchasing a miniature Dachshund from a breeder. The dog would be ready to be picked up in December.

    I think Gypsy had decided I would be his owner the moment he saw me. I was walking back to my apartment after picking up my mail and this dog started following me. I looked in his eyes and he looked right back at me. There was a connection. He made me smile.

    Gypsy followed me onto my small porch landing, looking emaciated and thirsty. I got a bowl (Tupperware…as I had no dog dish) of water for him and left it on the porch and went into my apartment, figuring he would go on his way. I looked out the window a few minutes later.  He was still there.  I could hear him lapping up the water in the bowl.  About a half hour later I went to retrieve the bowl and there he was, just sitting on the porch as if he belonged.  He looked at me with his one brown eye and his one blue eye and wagged his tail.  He looked starved, so I went inside and got the only thing I thought he could eat that I had……Ritz crackers.

While I was bringing the crackers outside to give him, I looked out the door and observed him staring into the apartment with his tail in the form of a question mark.  I had never seen that before and thought it was pretty neat.  I brought out the crackers on a plate and he devoured them and was in the apartment by the time my spouse, Christine, came home from work.  Before I let him into the apartment I sat on the porch with him for a few minutes.  He kept leaning into me.  That was it we had bonded.

Because he was a stray we had to leave him at the pound for 10 days in case anyone claimed him.  The dog officer stated that Gypsy (I named him after about 20 minutes of contemplation as he raced around the apartment) had been 'thrown away' by someone before and it was unlikely that he would be claimed. I went and visited him at the pound and got a big smile from him when we picked him up on the tenth day. From that day forward he was my constant companion.

Gypsy followed me everywhere....and I mean everywhere. From the moment I woke up until I went to sleep he was my constant companion. The only time I did not see him was when I was at work. He was my constant companion, my running buddy. When I woke in the morning he would sit on my legs while I was still in bed and stare at me. I would look back at him and start my daily question to him, "Would you like to go for a walk?" I got as far as "Would you" and he was off the bed, running around the room in constant motion, only stopping to allow me to clip the leash onto his harness. He would start 'talking' to me, not barking, but with a variety of sounds that I thought were his 'dog words'. Then we were off on our run. Gypsy would have the biggest smile on his face.

Have you ever made your dog smile....or laugh at you? All you have to do is do something ridiculous to get a response. My unforgettable moment was taking Gypsy with me when I went cross-country skiing through the woods across the street from our house. A fresh snowfall had given us over a foot of snow. The storm had ended, and a cold, sunny day lay ahead. As I got myself ready, Gypsy was jumping up and down, impatient for us to 'get going'. I finally got my ski's on and up and down hills we went...over streams and under big branches with Gypsy occasionally running across my ski's just to make sure I was okay. I was okay until my ski tip caught a branch and I went tumbling down a hill, somersaulting at least twice. Covered in snow from head to toe, I brushed the snow off of my face and opened my eyes. Gypsy's face was about 1 foot away, and that's when he smiled, or laughed, at me, licked my face and dashed around me waiting for me to get up. I laughed until my stomach hurt, and then struggled to untangle myself from the pretzel I had turned my body into. Gypsy moved close to me, gave me another kiss and I grabbed his harness to help pull myself up. We continued on our way for about another hour, returning home wet, exhausted, happy, and with a story to tell that I could not describe without breaking into uncontrollable laughter. A most treasured memory.

    There are times we spend with our dogs when we can sense their mood, almost as well as they sense our emotions. The emotional bond between a dog and its owner is difficult to describe. Yes, they do know when you are sad. How can you explain the nudge you get from a wet nose when you are feeling blue? Or the jump up onto the couch-and-lean-into-you move when they know you need a friend?

There are many other times when Gypsy made me smile. After Gypsy had lived with us a few weeks it was apparent that he needed training. Actually we needed the training too. We went to "Obedience School" that was in the basement of a building and there were about 6 other dogs there as well. On the first day of class we arrived and Gypsy proceeded immediately to the pole in the center of the room and peed, and peed, smiling at me the whole time. While I cleaned up after him, he decided to 'make friends' with several of the other dogs (who were much more under control)

Shortly after that we got another lesson in owning a dog. Coming home after leaving him in the apartment for a few hours (this was before we knew we needed to fence off an area or get a crate for him) we discovered dollar bills left on the coffee table chewed to bits, sea shells that we had collected, and the covers of a few books strewn about the living room floor. In the middle of it all was my Gypsy, with his big smile…..so happy to see us!

Gypsy had many nicknames. 'Special', because he had eyes with different colors, 1 blue and 1 brown. He was a Heinz 57, a mixed breed. We also called him Gypjap and Gypasee. The first year was very challenging for us as he was a bit wild. Gypsy had been with us for several weeks when one day I took him for a walk in the woods behind the apartment house. He kept bending down and eating something. I noticed there were crab apples on the ground everywhere. I didn't think much of it at the time but we soon found out that Gypsy had eaten some of them. That night he started crying to go out. He had the 'runs'! Needless to say we didn't get much sleep that night and took turns taking Gypsy out every hour to 'go'. After a couple of days he was okay but Gypsy always had stomach problems and we tried many different types of food over the years, finally settling on a raw food diet which his system accepted.

Gypsy and I used to love to go for runs together. While I was working at Milton Academy we lived in an apartment in a house on campus. At the back of the house there were woods and playing fields for sports. We often ran the fields, with me letting go of the leash as he dashed around, running so fast his back paws would be in front of his front paws. Well, one Saturday morning Gypsy got out as I went to put his leash on. He was so excited and he took off towards the fields. I didn't think too much of it until I went around the corner after him and saw there was a soccer game going on. "Uh-oh" I thought. And sure enough, there was Gypsy sprinting all over the field. He had stopped the game and nobody could catch him. Suddenly, he ran to the very middle of the field and squatted. The crowd that was at the game made a collective groan and I said "oh no". Gypsy finished his poop, heard me yell his name and sprinted for the woods, where I was able to finally get him under control. Having been embarrassed at our first dog training session, I wasn't about to be humiliated on the soccer field by going and cleaning up his mess. I was finally able to get him to follow me back to the apartment and made a mental note to check the sports schedule so that we wouldn't interfere with a game again!

I remember one time we went away for a few days and my Aunt Sandra, who lived in nearby Holbrook, took care of him for us. She would stop by the apartment, take him out and feed him. She had made some hot dogs for herself to eat and had left them on the counter while she went in the living room to get something. She went to get her hotdogs and one was gone! Gypsy had very quietly taken one and gobbled it down.

I have so many great memories of my Soul Dog. I remember after we moved to Holland, Massachusetts, he became friends with the neighbor's dog, Pepper. Unfortunately Pepper showed Gypsy where the swamp was and a few times he came running home covered in muck. We had to hose him down before he could go in the house. A bath followed. He didn't like that bath very much but that didn't stop him from visiting the swamp again.

Gypsy lived to the age of 17, rest in peace my buddy.

Gypsy

**DISNEY**

Disney was the only dog we owned that was not a rescue. He was a short-haired black and tan miniature Dachshund who had a variety of nicknames including Sir W. Disney, Mr. Wigglybutt, Dizzy, and Schmoo. He was always so happy! He would get so excited when he would greet people and his tail would wag so hard his whole entire back end would shake, giving him the 'wigglybutt' nickname.

When he was a puppy, he was so small his ears would touch the ground when he walked.

I remember the first night after we picked him up. He was only 8 weeks old. We tried to have him sleep in his crate but he kept crying. I had him sleep under my arm next to my heart. He feel asleep immediately. At night when we would go to sleep, Disney would always try to cuddle as close as possible to us. Yes, he slept on the bed too.

Disney had his issues. He often peed when he was nervous or when he saw my mother-in-law. She would say "Hi Disney" and he would roll over and start peeing. He never did that with anyone else.

One day we had gone out and left Disney and Gypsy in the house. When we came home we found them in a room off the kitchen batting a mouse around. It was alive and they had cornered it but did not kill it. I grabbed the mouse and took it outside. Setting it free, I thought quite highly of myself. What a good thing I was doing and I was also glad to get it out of the house. It was not the mouse's day though. As I watched it run across the yard, the neighbor's dog, Pepper, ran over to it, scooped it up in his mouth, and took off.

Disney definitely gave us some health scares and ended up being the most expensive dog we ever owned. He was good at getting into things. One time he got ahold of some chicken bones and started choking. We rushed him to the animal hospital and whatever he had swallowed was cleared from his windpipe so that he could breathe.

Disney ended up with a heart condition at age 6, and we had many trips to Tufts Animal Hospital to try to keep him alive. He passed away at the age of 9. It was a heartbreaking loss. We were all so sad. Gypsy was so depressed. They had been such good friends and had played together all the time. Disney would run up to Gypsy and hang on his fur or lie on him when he decided to sit down somewhere. They even played tug-of-war with rope bones. Since Gypsy was so much bigger than Disney, he would just gently hold the rope bone in his teeth while Disney pulled and yanked at the rope, trying to get it from Gypsy.

Disney will remain forever in our hearts.

**BRITTANY**

Brittany was a long-haired dapple miniature Dachshund. She was given to us with Nicodemus, a long-haired black and tan dachshund. Our friend Pam Patterson called us after Disney died, asking if we could take the dogs, as their owner, a family friend we always called Grandma DeBus, was having some health issues and could no longer take care of them.  Brittany was also Disney's sister and we decided to take them.  We immediately thought that having 4 dogs would be too much to handle but we knew the dogs well and wanted them with us.  We had also met them several times on previous visits to see Pam and Grandma DeBus.   It was comforting to us to be able to help take care of both Brittany and Nicodemus aka, Nicky.

    The first thing we did when we got them home was to give each a bath as they smelled like cigarette smoke as Grandma DeBus was a chain-smoker.
Brittany had many nicknames including the following:  little girl, Sassy Lassy, Queen of the House, pretty Britty, Tazmanian Devil.  From the first day she arrived, Brittany,  all 7 pounds of her, ruled the house.  She immediately got comfortable with her surroundings and had no fear of the other dogs.  She had a shrill bark and when she wanted something she let us know it.  Brittany also did whatever she wanted and could be stubbornly noncompliant, especially when it came time to clip her toenails.  It took 2 of us to get this task completed.  She was the 'tazmanian devil' when she knew if was nail clipping time!  I would have to wrap her in a

towel and offer her dog treats to distract her while my spouse, Chris, clipped her toes. She had the ability to contort herself and it was quite a challenge although the treats did distract her enough so that we could get each paw done.

    Brittany did whatever she wanted, including eating dog poop....her own and others. It was gross! I don't know what makes some dogs do that but we quickly learned to clean the yard by doing 'poop patrol' when we let her out. Eventually Brittany stopped this disgusting habit. However, with 4 dogs we were always cleaning up after them. Brittany became our helper in finding poop before we stepped in it. She would saunter over to a pile we missed and would sniff and then wait for us to clean it up.

    As Brittany aged she started to go blind. When we fed the 4 dogs, she would often take a few bites of her meal and then head over to Gypsy's dish, which was much bigger and had a lot more food. Gentle Gypsy would back away and look at us with that "help me out here" look. Eventually she developed symptoms of dementia, barking at all hours, staring at a wall and wagging her tail, and not eating. She was a very sweet dog who was on antibiotics for a very long time. Brittany was a very resilient little girl.   She passed away at 17.

**NICODEMUS**

Nicodemus, aka Nicky, was a long-haired black and tan miniature dachshund who, came from Pennsylvania along with Brittany. He was 6 years old when he arrived at our house. Over the years he was given many nicknames including the following: Little Man, Nicnac, Picnik, Pikpac, and Sir Lickalot.

We had recently lost Disney and had rescued a miniature dachshund (Petey) from the Dachshund rescue league. Our shepherd-husky mix, Gypsy, was lonely and we thought another dog would cheer him up (and us too!)

Nicky was extremely shy and had the most difficult time adjusting to his new environment. In the first month he did not leave his house very often, only to eat or go out to pee/poop. It took him awhile to warm up to us but eventually he was often sitting on my lap or next to me as much as possible. The four dogs got along very well. Nicky would occasionally lash out at Petey or Brittany. Sometimes it was because he was protecting his food. Other times it was for no reason at all. It was during one of these times when Nicky went after Petey that I received the one and only dog bite I ever experienced. Petey was walking by Nicky's house, which was located in our kitchen. I was there getting something out of the refrigerator when I saw Nicky charge Petey, growling and barking. Petey was shrieking and I stepped in to intervene, trying to push Nicky away. He bit me on the hand and immediately ran away. I scolded him and went to clean my hand up as it was bleeding and clearly swollen where the teeth marks were. I got cleaned up and went to find Nicky. He was in his house, clearly feeling guilty about biting me. Eventually he came out of his house and jumped up on the couch and sat with me. He seemed to be apologizing in his own way. I was never bitten again and the spats between Nicky, Brittany, and Petey were extremely rare after that incident. It was interesting that when Gypsy and Brittany passed away and it was only Petey and Nicky left, they got along great. I think they got used to each other and were not competition for attention as much.

Nicky became my constant companion, following me everywhere and crying to be placed on the couch next to me. As he aged he cried for everything (to be put on couch, food, etc.) I never had to look at the clock to know that it was time for dinner as Nicky would always start to cry about 10 minutes before it was time to eat. He was never much of a barker, always the quiet, unpredictable one.

One other habit that Nicky had was a tendency to lick everything. Also known as Sir Lickalot, Nicky's tendency to lick anything was a problem as we didn't want him to lick EVERYTHING so we had a 'lick towel' for him when he sat on the couch or bed.

One of my most treasured memories of Nicky was when we were staying at our friends Lydia Walz and Lizi Brown's while we waited to move into our new house. We had sold our house and had no place to live for a couple of weeks. With 4 dogs, we were fortunate to find friends that could help us out.

My friend Lydia was not a dog person and Nicky was not a people person. Yet, they sat together. The picture on page 150 was taken about 6 weeks before Lydia passed away, before any of us knew she was sick. She had esophageal cancer and by the time she was diagnosed, it was too late. I always think Nicky knew. Dogs have a way of sensing things we don't.

Nicky also ended up getting Cancer, mostly on his face and throat. He never complained but had difficulty eating. I fed him pumpkin pie filling, tunafish, graham crackers, and anything I was eating. I would chew it up and feed it to him like mama birds do for their chicks. Eventually Nicky's tumors grew and he was in a lot of pain. The pain medication didn't seem to be working and he stopped eating. It was clear that he was failing. He was suffering and we new it was time for him to be put down. Despite knowing that we were ending his suffering, it was still very difficult and I cried for days.

Nicky also lived to 17.

**PETEY**

Petey is my last angel (for now).  He came to us when he was 3 years old.  After Disney died we were looking for another Dachshund to give Gypsy a companion and hopefully help his depression.  We went to the Dachshund Rescue in Dartmouth, Massachusetts, where they had 8 dachshunds who had been driving there from the south.  Petey was from Tennessee.  We got there and I walked in and sat down on the floor.  Petey came right up to me and sat in my lap.  He found me.  We decided to keep him right then.

The background story we got on Petey was that he had been abused.  His previous owner had hit and thrown him.  The woman who owned him brought Petey to an animal shelter and said that she had to give him up because her husband was going to kill Petey.  Petey did show signs of abuse right from the start.  He was very afraid, watching our hands constantly, and was very tense when he was picked up.  Chris and I were the only people that could pick him up.  When we took him to the vet one of us would always have to go back with the vet tech when they would take blood or he would freak out, pooping and peeing all over them.  One time one of the vet tech's insisted on taking him by herself.  We said it was not a good idea but she insisted. A few minutes later she came storming out to the front of the office with pee on her and said "I think you should come back here". We smiled and said I told you so.

Petey had health issues early on. His nutrition was poor and he had an enzyme issue, where his body did not process food very well and he had a difficult time gaining weight. It took us a while to get his health issues sorted out but he has been a very healthy dog.

Petey got along great with Gypsy. When they first met. Gypsy ran up to him wagging his tail. I think he thought it was Disney. When he realized it wasn't his favorite buddy, his tail dropped and he walked away. However, he quickly became used to Petey and they spent a lot of time together. They never fought.

Petey was an anxious dog and as he aged his anxiety increased. He is the last of our 4 dogs and now that he is alone he is constantly looking for us. He doesn't like being alone at all.

You'll read much more about Petey including several stories about his adventures.

Petey

# PART II:
# 4 PAWED ANGEL TALES

Disney & Gypsy

Gypsy, K.G. Keough-Huff, & Disney

# Abuse, Neglect and Forced to Endure

## ABUSE

"Say Uncle!" he said. I was 9 years old. He was 14 years old. I was in the woods between our house and the neighbors. He chased me down, knocked me over onto my back, and sat on top of me. He pinned my arms up over my head and grabbed the pinkie finger on my right hand. "SAY UNCLE!" he yelled again. "NO!" I cried. His friend was there and I think he was trying to prove how tough he was. His friend said, "C'mon, leave her alone, she's just a kid." "SAY UNCLE!" he screamed loudly. He pulled my pinkie finger away from my hand. By this time I had started crying but I still said "NO." He bent it further and there was a small cracking sound. I cried out in pain. He looked at me in shock, got off me and said to his friend, "Let's go" and they ran off. I have a very vivid memory of this but I don't remember ever telling my mother what happened. My finger was swollen, I told her I fell, and she taped my ring and pinkie finger together. It is still a little crooked today.

  I used to voice my complaints but in a busy household, they were ignored. I learned that complaining invited more abuse so I learned to endure. I carried this pattern of coping into adulthood where it manifested itself in some of my early relationships and in my toleration of harassment and abuse in the workplace.

I was never physically abused at work but went through a period of time when I was working at Amherst when I was threatened and harassed verbally in meetings, in the hallway at school, and on the phone in my office. I even had anonymous hate letters sent to my home. When I complained at work, the harassment escalated. I remember meeting with the building Principal, who said to me, "Everybody hates you." He offered no support and did nothing to change the hostile climate I was encountering. The local police and school district human resource director provided no assistance. It only got worse. So I fell into my old pattern of enduring poor treatment. I kept thinking, "If I just work a little harder, it will get better, or it will go away."

My sister Pam likened my response to abusive behavior to the 'frog in the water analogy.' When a frog is thrown into hot water it immediately tries to escape, recognizing the danger. When a frog is placed in warm water that is slowly heated, it doesn't notice the danger until it is too late. The danger I ran into caused me to develop anxiety. My only escape was to jump out (or in this case I got pushed out). I reflect back on this experience and am grateful I survived.

The reason I share my own stories of abuse with you is because 2 of the dogs I have owned were rescue dogs that had been abused. I think dogs that are abused experience or exhibit some of the same behaviors. They learn to endure. A dog is mistreated, complains, and is punished again. So they endure. I can't imagine the horrific torture some dogs are forced to endure. I remember reading a Sports Illustrated article about the football quarterback who had a dogfighting compound. It made me nauseous reading what this murderer did to his dogs.

Gypsy was abused. When he came to us he had been neglected and was starving. When we first got him he always crawled under the bed at night and slept there. He was always very friendly but growled when he was around some men. Whoever had owned him prior to us did not treat him well.

Susan Rogers, dog trainer and kennel owner, tells a story of a dog she took in. "She was a 1 year old who had been neglected. She did not know words, even her own name."

Susan felt the dog may have been autistic or had suffered some type of brain damage. "It took her a long time to get her to be comfortable with being approached, patted, or held. She never showed joy or learned any social skills that other dogs learn. "

    My friend Diane Mossa, never had a dog while she was growing up or when she was working. Diane had retired and moved in with her parents to take care of them. A year after her mother died, one of her neighbors told her about a dog that was tied up outside all the time. One of Diane's neighbors asked the owner if he wanted to have someone take the dog. After numerous complaints about neglect, the owner agreed to give the dog up.

    The neighbor thought Diane needed a dog for company and brought her over to see it. "He was so sad looking," Diane said. "I brought him over to my Dad. It took him about a half hour to warm up and that's how I got Bailey. He lived with me for 13 years. He was with me when my Dad died. He was with me when my brother died. He was very good company, and although he wasn't a therapy dog, he was good therapy!"

Diane Mossa & Bailey

## ANXIETY – FEAR – STRESS

In her book "Live A Flourishing Life", author Rita Schiano writes about anxiety: "While a certain level of anxiety is considered normal, even beneficial, when the fear or apprehension becomes chronic, irrational, and interferes with life functions it is time to consider professional assistance.  Avoidance behavior, incessant worry, and loss of concentration and memory problems often stem from excessive anxiety.  Excess anxiety includes physical responses, such as heart palpitations and digestive disruption, distorted thoughts, excessive worrying and behavioral changes, such as being argumentative or withdrawing from social contact."

We all have anxiety and anxious moments in our lives.  When I was younger and participated in competitive sports, I remember being anxious before games.  As a college goalkeeper in lacrosse, I think the anxiety helped me to stay focused, and definitely got me pumped up and prepared for the pummeling I would endure in practice and in games.  Later, when I started coaching, I became anxious before games and tried to keep it from affecting my ability to communicate with and motivate the athletes I coached. Although I had to keep the nervousness in check, it helped me to prepare for competition and to handle the pressure that came with coaching.

    Anxiety never became a problem until I took a job as an administrator in Amherst, Massachusetts. The demands of the job were difficult with increasing responsibilities matched by decreasing budget and lack of support. After 2 years of this I was having an increasingly difficult experience with the way I was being treated at work. My clerical help had been cut and my year round position had been reduced to 10 months. Each week I would have a meeting with an administrator at the high school. He demanded that I create an agenda of items to discuss each week, which I did. Unfortunately, he would glance at the agenda, and would then launch into whatever he wanted to talk about. The conversations were often nonproductive and repetitive (he would often repeat comments he had made the previous week). During the last couple of years I was there he would periodically make some derogatory comment near the end of our meeting. I clearly remember him saying to me "Everybody hates you", and another time "I'd bank my reputation over yours anytime". These comments stunned me. They came out of nowhere and I did not know how to respond. At the end of each meeting he would take his copy of my agenda, rip it up and toss it in his recycling bin while I was there! He treatment of me was demeaning, demoralizing, and humiliating.

  I had worked for some really great leaders over the course of my career, so I knew the difference between excellent and poor leadership. He used bullying, threats, and intimidation regularly. Yet I allowed this to continue for several years. I really didn't have anyone to turn to for help in what was an increasingly bad situation.

  Unfortunately my anxiety increased and I began to develop physical symptoms that included nausea, vomiting, and stomach pain. Each week I would prepare for the meeting and my symptoms would begin a couple of hours before the meeting. There were several times that I went to the nurse's office to use one of their bathrooms because I was gagging and didn't want anyone to know I was throwing up. I tried all the stress reduction, anxiety-reducing exercises, and meditation to relieve the symptoms and it helped but the dreaded meetings continued until I left. Even though my departure was forced and extremely stressful, I felt tremendous relief upon leaving such a dysfunctional environment!

    I have had one anxiety attack since I left and it was because we were traveling home from a family party and got rerouted through Amherst. The road we usually take was shut down due to an accident and we were forced to go through Amherst. As we neared the school where I had worked, my chest tightened and I could not breathe. My wife became alarmed and asked me what was wrong. I was having a panic attack! My concerned spouse spoke calmly with me and after several minutes I finally relaxed as we exited Amherst. I was surprised that I had this reaction after more than 3 years had passed. Sometimes damage that is done takes a long time to heal and does not always go completely away.

    I can relate to dogs who are anxious. I know how they feel. My sister Christine had a German Shepherd named Cassie. Cassie had extreme anxiety, which she displayed by constantly chasing her tail and biting it. No amount of training or medication seemed to help. Her tail was constantly bleeding and became infected. Surgery to remove her tail became necessary. It was very sad but with aging, medication, and lots of love, Cassie's anxiety diminished. It still was there but was not so extreme.

As humans we learn coping strategies, such as meditation, to deal with our anxiety. Sometimes medication is needed as well. Dogs don't really have the coping skills to recover from anxiety. Sometimes their anxiety may diminish but something may trigger an anxious response and often only medication can relieve their condition.

Dogs respond to our anxiety too. When we become stressed they can become anxious as well. Paying attention, patting, playing, sitting with them can de-stress you and your dog.

Rufus and Maggie are both dogs that have been rescued. I spoke with my niece Samantha about them and how they have adapted to their new home over time. "When we first got Rufus we used to find him in the bathtub, shaking. He felt comfortable there and that had been his go to place with his previous owner. With lots of love and attention, Rufus got used to us and he started sleeping on the bed and we broke him of the habit of thinking we would be mad at him if he got on the bed. "

Rufus

Dogs who have been neglected or abandoned can become stressed very easily. Dogs who have been rescued can often arrive with many issues that trigger their anxiety. Our most anxious dog was our rescue dog, Petey.

Petey's anxiety became obvious to us within the first few days of being brought to our home, and has been exhibited in many different ways over the years. He was terrified of being picked up.

For weeks and months after he came to live with us he watched our hands. He came to trust us gradually, realizing that our hands would not hurt him. Some of his fears went away as he became more comfortable in his new house and with the people and animals he interacted with. However, we always had to carry him or be with him when he saw the vet. He would totally freak out if one of the vet aides tried to take him for blood work. They always let us go back with them while he had blood drawn or tests so that they could avoid the crying, peeing and pooping he would do if we were not there

Over time Petey built up his trust in us and his fear became less of an issue, but has always remained on some level. As he has aged he has become more anxious, especially when we have to leave. When Petey joined us he had other dogs around him. The others have all passed away and he is the only one left. We put him in his dog crate when we would go out and he often peed or pooped in his crate, something that he did not do when we had the other dogs. It didn't matter if we took him out to 'do his business' before we left. It didn't matter if we were gone for 30 minutes, or for 4 hours, Petey still peed.

As Petey's vision, hearing, and other faculties decline, he has become more fearful. He cries and wants to be comforted more often. Old fears have returned and new one's have emerged.

I think I understand Petey's anxiety issues and have more patience with him because of my own anxiety. Petey was treated badly and thrown away. So was I. In the end we both got out of a very bad situation and are much better off today.

As dogs and people age, they become more fearful. Especially when we start to lose those senses that we rely on throughout the day, like vision, hearing, and balance. "I've fallen and I can't get up." We used to laugh at those commercials but as we start to age and feel the effects of not being able to depend on our senses, so does the reality that this could happen to us. So we limit our risks. We go out less, think before we take action (sometimes) if we want to maintain good health. The reckless abandon of youth is life-threatening in old age.

As Petey has aged some of those fears have come back, and new ones have emerged as well. His fear of abandonment has increased as the other dogs in our house have passed away. He cries when he doesn't know where we are. We noticed this has increased after he lost his other dog buddy, Nicky, who passed away. He also has frequent "accidents". Part of this is his doggy dementia but it is also the fear he feels when we are not there.

I have a friend, Kristen, who credits her dog Rorie, with saving her life. She had lived with her parents for a long time due to a disability. Kristen had grown up with dogs and really wanted to get a dog after she was able to move out and be on her own. Kristen was suffering from anxiety and depression when her sister found Rorie on a website and encouraged Kristen to pursue adoption. "Nobody thought I could have a dog. Rorie was a breeder dog that had been put up for adoption at age 3. They were done with her. She had had 4 litters. I had her flown in from Nevada and I picked her up at Bradley International Airport in Hartford, Connecticut.

When I got her home she peeked out of her pen and kissed my cheek. She then peed for 5 minutes. I timed it!" Kristen goes on to talk about the impact that Rorie has had on her life: "Since I got Rorie I came off my medications. The exercise and companionship, and being responsible for her has helped me tremendously. Rorie is not qualified as a therapy dog but she really is. I would have days when I would cry and not want to get out of bed, and Rorie would nudge me, wake me up. I have become more independent. I have branched out. I am more confident. "

"I wish Rorie was classified as a therapy dog because with my anxiety I would go out and do more if I could bring her with me. She definitely helps me with my anxiety because I am focused on her."

"Rorie came to me with her own anxiety. We had this instant bond. I needed her and she needed me. We have our routine. I come home from work and she is waiting for me. I take her for a walk and she acclimates her walk to keep my pace."

## SADNESS/GRIEVING – DEPRESSION - CRYING

Dogs are extremely sensitive. They have an acute sense of our feelings of sadness, grieving, and depression. They often react by trying to console us when we cry. Susan Rogers, dog trainer and owner of Stirling Kennels, described one of her dogs demonstrating an acute case of sadness over a loss. Susan's dog, Gillis, had just turned 14 and had cancer. Her other dog Jack had come to live with them a few years earlier and was Gillis' best buddy. Gillis passed away and Jack didn't eat after she died. Jack died 9 days after Gillis from no known cause.

Susan also described the relationship that one of her dogs had with a Siamese cat they had. The two had been together for several years. They traveled west together and came back east. At one of the rest stops, the cat was stolen. Susan says, "If we even thought about the cat, the dog would go to the window in the living room and cry. It got to the point where we had to stop mentioning or thinking about her because it stressed the dog too much."

After our first dog Disney died, Gypsy used to walk around the house looking for him. He was so sad and quiet. I think he really missed his friend. I sensed he also felt our sadness over losing Disney as well.

Sensing the sadness of another can be powerful - and sometimes overwhelming, as happened when my father came to watch a game at the school that I worked. My father loved baseball and over several years I had taken him to some of the baseball games at the schools I worked at. I was working in Amherst, Massachusetts and the team had made the playoffs. My father hadn't been to a game yet, so I asked him and he was excited to go.

We were seated near the spectator's rooting for Amherst when a student got a little out of control, screaming and making obscene gestures towards players on the other team. I went to speak with the student to settle him down so that he wouldn't get thrown out or escalate the situation. While I was talking to him, students and parents started yelling at me, spewing hateful homophobic comments and swearing at me the entire time. The student listened to what I had to say, apologized to me and returned to his friends. I started back towards my seat. I glanced at the front row of the bleachers and saw at least 6 of my colleagues and administrators just sitting there smiling at me. None of these adults intervened and nobody came to my defense.

I walked back to my seat, hoping my father hadn't heard what they had said. The look on his face told me that he had heard it all. I will never forget the sadness in his eyes. He said, "I wish you had never taken this job." I'm sure if he were alive today he would be very glad that I don't work there anymore. He was disgusted with the behavior of the adults who were yelling at me. He never went to another baseball game with me, which was really sad because it was one of the things we enjoyed doing together.

Dogs can be sad for many reasons and can even become depressed just like humans. They grieve when they lose a person or other animal friend. Rita Schiano describes a dog's grieving when she spoke with me about her dogs Jazzy and Frisco. Jazzy was a lab mix while Frisco was a shepherd mix. "I would put them out on the deck while I went to work. I came home one day and Frisco came in very slowly. Jazzy walked into the house slowly and then collapsed. I had to carry her out the door. I was trying to get her in the car and I was calling for help because I couldn't lift her and get the car door open. I finally got her to the veterinarian's office. I had to leave her there as "Dr. Mac", who takes care of my dogs was not there. Shortly after I got home, Dr. Mac called. He happened to stop by the clinic and saw that Jazzy was there. He told me he was going to stay with her. She had lost a lot of blood and wanted to see if she had been poisoned. Her heart had stopped. Dr. Mac told me "Rita, I am so sorry. She had another heart attack and we couldn't save her. "

Dr. Mac did an autopsy and found that Jazzy wasn't poisoned but had suffered an aneurism. Rita says, "When I got home Frisco was lying on the spot where Jazzy collapsed. She would not move from that spot!"

"Frisco needed another dog. She grieved deeply when Jazzy died. She grieved for months. I knew I had to get another dog. Frisco wouldn't eat any food, she was losing her fur, and was epileptic as well.

One day Dr. Mac called and said that they have a dog that would be perfect for her. I named her Satche. She was a chow and golden retriever mix. I said to her, "do you want to come home with me?" She sat in my lap and that was it. I brought her home and I called Frisco. Satche walked in and Frisco wagged her tail and was so excited. They were great friends for many years."

**DEPRESSION**

Muppet

    Dogs can suffer from depression just like people do. There are varied stages of depression that I have seen both in people and in dogs. When someone has experienced the loss of a loved one or other trauma, stomach upset, not eating, and overwhelming sadness are symptoms of depression that can occur.

    Our first 2 dogs, Gypsy and Disney, were buddies for nine years. When we lost Disney to a heart condition, Gypsy started to exhibit signs of depression. Whether he was experiencing our sadness or not, he definitely carried his own sadness, wandering around the house looking for Disney. Gypsy became much quieter and less active, lying down and looking so sad. After a few months we decided to look for another dog to keep Gypsy company and for us as well. We found the Dachshund rescue league and brought Petey home. He was a 3 year-old who happened to look a lot like Disney but had his own personality and lots of issues.

      Gypsy's depression (and ours) lifted almost immediately when Petey entered our lives. We missed Disney terribly but Petey filled a void and was a good companion for Gypsy. It took Gypsy a little while to warm up to Petey though. When we brought Petey home and put him on the kitchen floor, Gypsy ran up to him, wagging his tail. I think he thought it was Disney. One sniff and the tail stopped wagging. Petey froze and Gypsy sniffed a little more, put his head down, dropped his tail and walked away. Gradually they became friends and several months later we added two more dogs (Nicky and Brittany), who were given to us by an elderly friend who could not take care of them any longer.

Nicky and Brittany were both miniature Dachshunds. Brittany was 9 years old and Nicky was 6 years old. Brittany was very outgoing and soon became the Queen of the house. It took a long time for Nicky to get comfortable in his new home. I think he was very stressed and depressed about the sudden change of moving into a strange house with new people. Gradually, he warmed up to us but it took awhile. For almost a month, he would only leave his crate to 'do his business' and eat his dinner. He also snapped at the other dogs as well. Finally he joined us on the couch and he became one of my constant companions. If I settled down on the couch to watch TV or read, the dogs would arrive and arrange themselves around and on me. Gypsy at my feet, Petey next to my right thigh, Nicky next to my left thigh, and Brittany sitting on my lap, where they napped until I either got up or they heard or saw something that distracted them.

    I have another sister, Cindy Craig, who has suffered from depression for many years. Cindy had a dog named Muppet that she had taken in when Muppet was a few years old. Muppet became Cindy's constant companion. She was a gentle soul and Cindy took great care of her. When Muppet passed away Cindy was depressed for a while and then eventually came out of it. Cindy said "A year after Muppet died I was feeling really depressed and couldn't think what the trigger could have been. Then I realized that it was around the same time that Muppet had died." Muppet was most likely Cindy's soul dog, and her loss is still felt, especially on the anniversary of her passing.

I think all people have the potential to suffer from depression. Loss of a loved one, job loss, a breakup in a relationship can all trigger depression. Sometimes we are sad for a few days. Sometimes it lasts weeks and even months. We need help when it interrupts our ability to function. Not eating, excessive sleep, and withdrawing from the world, are all symptoms that many people exhibit when suffering from depression. Most people bounce back but there are many who need help to recover and don't get the help they need. Wouldn't it be great if we could end a person's depression by giving them a new companion, like we sometimes do with dogs?

My friend Diane Mossa has two Shih Tzu's named Bandit and Zeus. They are brothers but have very different personalities. "Zeus is very aggressive when we are outside. When we go inside, he won't go upstairs, which Bandit will do. I got Bandit and Zeus from someone who had left a bad marriage. I think the dogs were exposed to a bad situation. They have adapted really well to living with me. They are very protective of each other and understand my emotions. We take in the New Year together. They are my constant companions. As a result, I don't feel lonely. When I got them I was going through a period in my life when lots of friends and family passed away. I was not feeling up to par physically and mentally. Bandit and Zeus really helped me through this difficult time."

Bandit & Zues

## CRYING

One day we had left our four dogs (Gypsy, Petey, Nicky, and Brittany) at the house while we went out to dinner with friends. Usually we just get in the car and go but this time our friends picked us up. We decided to wait outside on our front steps so that they wouldn't have to ring the doorbell. This allowed us to avoid the chaos that the dogs created whenever someone arrived at the door.

We sat quietly on the steps. After a couple of minutes, there was a quiet and low howl coming from the house. Gypsy, our shepherd/husky mix began to howl long and loud. He was quickly joined by the 3 dachshund's high-pitched howls. So long and mournful! We had no idea they did this when we left. We laughed quietly until tears were streaming down our faces. We had discovered that they really miss us when we are gone. The howling went on for several minutes and then stopped as suddenly as it began. They had each other to keep company I guess.

I can only think of 2 instances when a person cries like this. The wailing of a person in grief over the loss of a loved one or a baby crying. I can also remember when my nieces or nephews would come to visit for a few days. When it was time to leave they would start to cry. I always took it as a compliment, thinking they must have had a good time.

### PASSIVE/AGGRESSIVE

It is very difficult to deal with people who have passive/aggressive personalities. In my experience with individuals with this behavior, I have been fooled and damaged by their antics. I view these types of people as dangerous and steer clear of them when I recognize their pattern of behavior. One should always be wary around individuals who are smiling on the outside but behind your back are saying and acting in ways that can hurt you. With dogs that are passive aggressive you should be careful too. However, dogs can usually be trained to eliminate this behavior whereas people are unlikely to change.

Dorsie Kovac, veterinarian, described a client who was using intimidation, muzzling, and other dominating techniques to control their dog, a Rottweiler. "The dog became even more aggressive. The negative energy was intimidating and the training backfired, with the dog snapping back. We need to train people to build a relationship of respect with their dog through praise. Dominance techniques can make a dog more aggressive. It is better to train with positive reinforcement."

When Gypsy arrived at my house he was a wild, untrained 7 month-old stray. We signed up for training classes and I quickly learned that I was the one being trained. One of the habits that he came to us with was to jump on people. If you put your arm up, he would clamp his mouth on it. We think his previous owner was training him to be an attack or fighting dog so we needed to retrain him to end this behavior.

One of the techniques we were taught was called Dominance Down. It involved bringing the dog to the floor and lying on him and holding him to the floor. Gypsy wouldn't hurt a fly but I didn't want him jumping on people, so I tried it. Gypsy jumped and I brought him down on the carpet with one leg over his hips and my arms holding his head. He struggled and I didn't have a good grip and we ended up rolling across the floor. Gypsy thought it was a great game we were playing!

It took a few times to get this technique down but I think positive reinforcement is really what got him to stop jumping on people.

Nicky (Nicodemus) also displayed passive/aggressive tendencies. This behavior didn't occur very often and it was usually towards other dogs, not people. I remember one time Nicky was sitting quietly in the living room and one of our other dogs, Petey, walked by. Nicky, usually so quiet and docile, watched Petey pass and then lunged at him. Then WWIII dog style quickly broke out.

## ANGER

Anger is one of the many emotions dogs can express clearly and sometimes do. With a flash of teeth, hair raised up on their backs, and growling you know this dog is not happy. People show anger too. We don't flash our teeth but we express anger through our harsh eyes, shouting, and tense body language. I am one of those people who, unfortunately, gets angry once in awhile. It is usually something really minor that I overreact to. I tend to let things build up. As several situations occur that tick me off, I don't respond, but inside I am starting to boil. Then something happens, that last straw, and I blow.

Dogs can react that way too. I remember someone telling me a story about their dog never being angry. It suddenly snapped at some kids who were taunting him, which is probably a good reason to get angry.

I never remember any of my dogs being angry although Gypsy would sometimes growl at men.

## PAIN & SHOCK

Being in pain, chronic or acute, is miserable. I have had broken fingers, leg, ankle, and a herniated disc in my lower back that eventually required surgery. I was fortunate to have a wonderful spouse who took care of me when I needed help. My dogs took care of me too.

I remember when I was waiting for my back surgery I could not walk. I was in so much pain that I had to sleep in a lazy boy chair. Chris, my spouse, would get me coffee and an energy bar for breakfast. Then she would leave for work. The dogs would settle in around and on me. Petey slept on my right, Nicky slept on my left, and Brittany would lie on my lap. Gypsy would lie on the floor at my feet. I only got up to go to the bathroom. I would crawl on the floor with all 4 of them following me. They would watch me, and when I returned to my chair they would all settle back into their same spots. When I think back on that most difficult time, I am so grateful for their companionship.

    One day I let them out into our fenced in yard. They were always very good about coming inside when I called. Except for one day, Brittany decided she was going to stay outside. I was concerned that some animal or hawk might attack her as she was only 7 pounds. I crawled around the yard after her. When I would get a couple of feet away, she would run just far enough to get away. Brittany would then glance back at me, wagging her tail. She was playing a game! I was in excruciating pain and she wanted to play. I started to cry, then started to laugh hysterically. Eventually she got bored and came in the house.

    My angels were all very brave. I know that Gypsy was in pain because he could barely walk. At the age of 16, his hips were in bad shape, yet he never complained. No matter how difficult it was, wherever I went in the house, he would always try to follow me. My Soul Dog, who would run 5 miles with me when he was young and healthy, still wanted to go along with me. In the last few months of Gypsy's life, we ended up taking very short walks around the outside of the house.

    Nicodemus (Nicky) was in pain the last few months of his life. He had cancer. Nicky could barely eat, his tumor was so large, but he always tried. He would not eat his dog food but became fond of pumpkin pie mix, Gerber baby food, and anything I could get him to try. He was especially interested in anything I was eating so I would chew up my food and give it to him, taking it out of my mouth and feeding it to him by hand, like a mama bird feeding their babies.

    When Nicky stopped eating, he was so uncomfortable and started complaining constantly. The medication, which had helped with the pain, clearly was not effective any longer. We had to make the most difficult decision that any dog owner has to make. I grappled with the question of whether I was keeping him alive for me or is it time to end his suffering. When he went several days without eating we knew it was time. I still miss him so much.

I never used an electric fence with any of my dogs. I understand why they are used to protect dogs that live near busy streets, or from running away, or going after someone, or chasing a car. I could never use them because I know the pain that an electric shock can cause.

I remember when I was about 8 years old, my brother, the oldest at age 13, would take care of us when our parents went out to dinner. I had 2 older sisters and 1 younger sister. For some reason I was the target of my brother's teasing, or in this case tazing. My brother was pretty smart and creative. One time he created a 'zapper' that he would plug into the wall to charge. He would then chase me around the house to deliver an electric shock. It didn't kill me but it hurt and he succeeded in terrifying me.

When I read the stories about the NFL quarterback (criminals will remain nameless in this book) and how he used to beat and shock his fighting dogs, it made me nauseous. It also reminded me of that helpless feeling when I was young, being overpowered and hurt by someone who was supposed to take care of me. I dreaded the times when my parents would go out.

I forgave my brother a long time ago. He did scare me at times but he also protected me as well. I remember one time I fell out of a tree (about 10 feet). I couldn't breathe and was really scraped up and I remember him carrying me all the way home. Today, my brother and I have a good relationship. It took years to repair but I love him and know that he loves me too. Sometimes a protector, someone we look up to or admire, can also be abusive. My pattern of enduring abuse has had a lasting effect. Making changes in my life to break this pattern has been a life long challenge. Yet there is hope.

    I recently watched a video of hundreds of dogs being rescued from a farm where they had been neglected and abused. They had lived in deplorable conditions and some of the dogs were nearly dead. They were frightened and scared but over time many of the dogs recovered. Lots of love, care, and attention helped them to heal.

    Despite the suffering endured in previous chapters, we, and our four pawed friends prevail through forgiveness and healing.

# Making the Connection from Healing to Forgiveness – Who Rescues Who?

## TRUST/FAITH

I remember reading an article in the news about a town that had ordered a banner with the town insignia 'In God We Trust' printed on it. The banner came back with God spelled backwards and read 'In Dog We Trust'. The town decided to keep the banner as is.

Dogs have such faith and trust in us. Wouldn't it be great if we could have the same faith in God as our dogs have in us? While I am writing this I am thinking of my niece, Sarah, who has that level of trust in her relationship with God. I don't think many people have that these days. Maybe dogs can help us find that faith, just like they help us in so many other ways.

Dorsie Kovacs, veterinarian, feels that dogs giving kisses and licking have healing in mind. She says that when dogs lick a wound it heals faster. "They clean it up. There are enzymes in their saliva and cleaning it up is therapeutic as well. Our dog Gus could smell cuts through our clothes. He would sniff and sniff and then lick the area."

Dogs have a capacity for empathy. They sense our feelings and try to help. Sharon Johnson relates another story about

Gus, their Golden Retriever. "One night I got home at about 1:00 a.m. from work. I had been talking to a woman who was describing that she had to put her dog to sleep. I was really sad and thinking about this when I got in the house. Gus was looking down at me from the top of the stairs. He came over to me and kept nudging me. Gus had his stuffed animal 'babies' that he would take care of. I went to bed and the next morning I woke up and one of his babies was next to me."

## UNCONDITIONAL LOVE

When you come home, how happy they are to see you! I remember Disney used to wag his tail so hard his whole butt would shake. One of his nicknames ended up being Mr. Wiggly Butt.

Researchers have discovered that the same pheromone is given off when a dog greets you as when a person expresses love for you. No matter how bad our day is or what our mood is, dogs are so happy to see us when we arrive from wherever we've been. On almost every occasion I am greeted with a wagging tail, bright eyes, and the obligatory 'sniff down' to try to determine where I've been. If I have been near other dogs, the sniffing of my body takes a little longer.

Imagine having a person greet you like that every day. Yes, we can learn a lot from dogs about love. I think we may express unconditional love a dog shows most closely when we see someone we love and miss and haven't seen in awhile. I have felt this when running into an old friend and the years just melt away. Other times it's a special moment with my significant other, or holding a baby for the first time.

To be a recipient of unconditional love is the most wonderful experience. Too bad people are not often as capable as dogs for loving unconditionally. To provide this love is incredibly powerful. And risky. Risky because those we love unconditionally can also be the source of emotional pain. But wouldn't it be great to express ourselves the way dogs do every day?

Dogs can teach us a lot about love. Maybe they are closer to God than we are. We are told that God loves us unconditionally. And I believe this….some days. However, I know people who experience God's unconditional love the way we experience a dogs unconditional love. When I meet these people I am amazed at their faith.

My goddaughter, Samantha Doucette, was talking with me about her dogs, Maggie and Rufus, and the unconditional love and joy they express. "Every time we come home, from vacation, even from just being away a day, they show so much joy upon seeing us. One time we were coming back from vacation and we could hear them barking when we pulled into the driveway. Rufus would pee and Maggie would smile and wag her tail so her whole body shook."

I don't know that we ever express joy as often or as demonstratively as dogs do. Dogs have a very limited capacity compared to people. They don't have speech or limbs with fine motor skills. They do make the very most out of the capacity they do have. We can learn something from dogs on that! They can be so joyous daily, even more than once a day, whereas we tend not to express our joy at simple things, even really big things too. Imagine what it would be like if we did! For some people that first sip of coffee in the morning can bring joy but some might think it weird if you express your joy over a cup of coffee.

My dogs showed the same joy and unconditional love every day. It didn't matter what kind of day I had or what kind of mood I was in, they were always so thrilled I was home!

## SHOW DOGS

Susan Rogers is the owner of Stirling Kennels in Stafford, Connecticut. She has worked with dogs for most of her life. Besides boarding dogs, she also produces nutritious food for dogs. Throughout her life she has been a Dog Breeder and has entered her Airedales in Dog Shows all over the country, Susan is an amazing woman who has provided shelter, rescue, love, and training to hundreds, if not thousands, of dogs. She has also had an impact on the lives of the people who bring their dogs to her.

Susan had an interest in showing and caring for dogs at a very young age. Susan says, "My earliest memory was during WWII and being a 2 year-old walking beside an Airedale and holding onto its hair."

"When I was 4 years old my Aunt took me to my first dog show. We would summer in Plymouth and that is when I went. I remember standing beside the ring, holding onto the rope. At the end of the show I turned to my Aunt and said, "I am going to have one of those." (referring to Airedales)

"At the age of 13 my Grandfather gave me an Airedale. I showed in Obedience at age

14 or 15. My first show was the Springfield Kennel Club at the Big E. I won and got a 6 foot length leash as a prize."

"I currently breed dogs and show them at various shows around the country. I mentor people who are learning about breeding and showing dogs."

There is a decision-making process in selecting a dog to compete/show. Susan states, "You can talk with Breeders about what you are looking for and breed to that standard. Now I mentor people about breeding. People will talk with us about what they are looking for. It is more of a selection process then it used to be. The Internet has made the selection process international. Categories for show are looks, agility, obedience, hunting, tracking."

Susan had two dogs that were her favorite show dogs. "The first was a male, Geordie, born in 1965. I owned his mother and bred her and kept Geordie. I experienced terrible grief over losing him. The second was a female from Texas. What a character! A holy terror! Her name was Gillis and she had a number of children. She was a 'do everything' dog and she lived to the age of 14."

After working with dogs for many years, Susan decided to open a kennel for boarding dogs. "I ended up bringing my Kennel and business to Stafford, Connecticut because I needed more room. We lived in North Monson and a neighbor complained about the noise. We had a kennel for our own dogs, and then started the Boarding business.

We both worked as teachers as well. Shirley (Susan's partner) and I spent time teaching people how to care about dogs, caring for puppies. We also educated people about proper nutrition for dogs. Eventually I decided to leave teaching and focus on the kennel."

Operating the kennel has provided memorable negative and positive experiences.

"One thing that was disappointing was the people not willing to care for their dog. I remember a guy who brought in his Rottweiler. He was in a rush and didn't sign the papers and left. The dog was in bad shape. I checked on him 3 hours later and he had died. I wrapped her up and he came back. I was very angry and he acted indifferent. He didn't seem to care at all that his dog had died."

"Dogs were never a disappointment. People are the biggest disappointment when dealing with dogs. For example, people who kept their dog outside because they didn't want them to get the house dirty. I remember one time a guy came in with a dog that was sick and who nobody wanted to take in. He said, "Nobody would take her. She is going to die here but don't call me." I brought her outside and gave her some water. Her name was Isabel. "

"Dogs have been abandoned here. One was in such bad shape I had to have it put down. There are some people who throw away dogs if they become an inconvenience."

"There have been many positive and funny experiences with dogs. People learning how to handle dogs and training puppies can be hysterical. A positive and hilarious experience is having a litter of Airedale puppies racing around going crazy and just sitting and watching and laughing at them."

Susan offers this advice for someone who wants to show dogs for a career. "Showing dogs is for anybody at any age. It is good for young people to apprentice to learn about animal husbandry. They have the opportunity to learn and move about the country as they get to travel everywhere. It is an exciting new career for young people. "

"For Confirmation & Professional Handing, you can start as a junior handler as early as 6 years old. The training teaches them about respect for animals. They have to have good grades in school, display sportsmanship, and they learn to interact with people and dogs. No cell phones are allowed in learning how to train dogs. They learn all the nuances about dogs to make them look good."

## RESCUE ME

Two of my angels were "rescue dogs." Gypsy, the stray dog that nobody wanted, and Petey, given up by a woman who feared for his safety. They made it to us through luck, circumstance, and the wonderful work of those people who are dedicated to saving dogs. Foster homes for dogs are really important because dogs don't always show their personalities very well in a kennel. They are less anxious and display more of their character when they are in a home.

I have 2 friends, Heidi Knowlton and Raja Mukerjee, who have been foster parents for rescue dogs. Most of the dogs they rescue are Pit Bulls. They have repeated what many other people who work with dogs have said, "There are no bad dogs, just bad owners." They loved all the Pit Bulls that came into their home and helped find them forever homes. It is hard to keep a dog for a while and then give it up. Knowing that it is going to a good home makes it worthwhile. Some people even keep in touch with the foster parents, giving occasional reports on their progress and health. Heidi says "I used to be afraid of Pit Bulls. I was never around them but friends of mine in rescue talked about them. One person who volunteered at a shelter told me there were many Pit Bulls who came in that weren't adopted."

Heidi's first foster dog was a chocolate Labrador named Glob, who had been used as a breeder. Her original goal was to foster one dog. After Glob found a forever home, Heidi decided to continue fostering dogs. The president of the local rescue contacted her about fostering a Pit Bull puppy that someone wanted to surrender. Heidi described the interview as very dramatic. "I called the phone number and met the woman at her house. The female Pit Bull was 4 months old. The dog was the runt of the litter and was very small. She was black with white and brown spots. I got out the surrender form and they proceeded to answer the numerous questions about the dog's background. The dog hadn't bitten anyone and the interview was going fine until the woman's pregnant daughter walked in and started screaming – Don't give her to a shelter! They will put her down! I tried to reassure them she was in a foster home and would stay with me. The daughter stomped out of the room with her mother and father yelling at her."

Heidi brought the puppy Pit Bull home and named her Sassy. "She was quiet. I grew to love that dog."

Heidi eventually gave up Sassy and it was one of the most difficult experiences she has ever been through. "I was very particular about who would get to adopt her. I still think about her every day. We really bonded. Sassy also got along really well with my dog. When we get the applications we check all the references, and do a home visit. There were some applications that weren't up to snuff. For those I would email and ask them a ton of questions. That discouraged some from pursuing an adoption. Then this young couple called. The references were exceptional, all questions answered and we made arrangements for them to meet Sassy. They played with her for a while and decided that they wanted to keep her. Sassy had been with me for 3 months, and I'd seen her through an illness, and I just loved her. I was very torn as to whether or not I should give her up. My friend John Grabosky spent a lot of time with her. He adored Sassy. When I told him about the adoption, he said I was stupid and that I should keep the dog."

"Sassy was only my second foster dog. Experienced foster care director's say when you leave the foster dog at their new home, act cheerful not tearful, and to sound enthusiastic that they were getting the dog. We went to the home and took her with us. I tried not to get emotional. They had bought toys and a dog bed for her. I went to the door and Sassy tried to follow me. I found out later that she had stayed by the door all day long. After I left her, Raja and I decided to go to an art exhibit as a distraction. I had such anger over my decision and I cried every day for the next week. I missed Sassy so much. My own dog got depressed. "

Sometimes adopted dogs get to keep in touch with their foster parents. "We were able to see Sassy 2 more times but I haven't seen her for a long time. The couple broke up and I don't get to see Sassy anymore." Heidi said. Heidi is still fostering dogs and Sassy will always hold a special place in her heart.

During the research for this book I had the opportunity to interview Pam Alvarez, owner of Abby's Little Friends Dog Rescue in Naples, Florida. Pam started her own rescue in memory of her dog Abby. It is a rescue for small breed dogs and she has been operating the rescue for more than 6 years. Pam say's "Abby was a good girl. She had cancer at 6 years old and I had to put her down. It destroyed me."

"Kylie followed Abby. Animal control called and said they had 4 Shih Tzu's that were dropped off. I took one look at Kylie and decided she would be a keeper."

"Years ago, I had a Shih Tzu named J.B. that passed away. I was looking for another dog and heard there were rescue dogs and called the place to inquire about adopting. I never heard back so I decided to foster dogs myself."

Pam has seen it all when it comes to saving dogs. At my house right now I have 9 dogs, 2 are mine. They all get along. Trubes was my first foster dog. He was always growling and wouldn't let me hold him. He made lots of talk. I looked at him one day and said, Are you talking to me? And he did a 180. I could even pick him up. I never heard from the director about his history but did find out he had been tied to a table for 7 years. Nobody was interested in adopting him so I decided to keep him."

"Nobody wants to see dogs get old, "Pam says. "I took in Simon, a 4-pound Yorkie. He was terrified of people. The owners burnt him with cigarettes. It took me a year to get the dog to trust me."

"I had another Yorkie, a 12 year old with cataracts that clung to me. After a few days I knew something was wrong. I took her in and the vet said she had brain damage. The dog had punctured eardrums and had been thrown."

"I don't like people who just turn their dog in for no reason. It gets me mad. I have a dog that was surrendered because they had a toddler who was holding some food, which the dog took." Not a good reason to give up a dog. They shouldn't have had it in the first place."

"You get sad when they go. You get attached, you cry when they leave, some you do a happy dance when they are adopted." "I had a hurricane Katrina dog, a Shih Tzu named Buddy. He was in tough shape. His eyes were glued shut from an infection. I got him all better and took him out for adoption to a young couple. He walked to the car, turned and ran back to me, gave me some kisses, and ran to the car. I wept and was sad but at the same time was glad she was going to a good home."

"I have another dog, Mandy, who came to me with a broken pelvis. I have had her 3 years and she still doesn't like to be picked up. She will probably stay with me and not get adopted."

Pam gets some of the dogs from the Kyer County Animal Control in Miami. She takes in dogs that are not doing well at a shelter. "I have a dog Joey who was terrified at the shelter. I left him alone and he gradually warmed up to the others and me." Pam says, "I also have a Shih Tzu named Nicky, a 1 year old who was dumped." Pam added, "We try to take care of their medical needs. Right now I have Brady, and we are trying to save his eye.  He was so matted when he came in but he is such a nice dog."

    Pam has volunteers who help with foster care but she is very careful about who she allows to volunteer. "We take in sick dogs, dogs that are fine but the people don't want them any more.  We get them better and look for forever homes for them.  We take donations to cover expenses and the adoption fee varies but is usually around $350.  Every rescue is looking for foster homes.  There are dogs coming in constantly.  It is never ending.  To adopt you need to fill out an application, get a reference from a vet, 2 personal references, and have a home visit.  We have a 98.5% success rate."

    To make donations:  Abby's Little Friends Dog Rescue  3713 Springwood Dr. Naples, FL 34104  You can visit the website abby'slittlefriends.com

    Now that we are rescued and the healing and forgiveness has begun, we are ready to grow into loyalty and protection.

# Growing into Loyalty and Protection

**Gypsy & Disney**

## GENEROSITY

Dogs have taught me about generosity. What does being generous really look like? Dogs share their love, affection, and feelings with us, and don't ask for anything back. When we need their generous ear or affection, they are there for us. I can remember a time when I was grieving, having lost a close friend very suddenly. I was sitting on my couch crying silently and my "Soul Dog", Gypsy, walked up to me and put his head on my lap. I patted his head and he responded by jumping up on the couch, leaning into me as if to say, "I am here for you."

Gypsy was also very generous to other dogs. At one time we had 4 dogs, 3 miniature Dachshunds and Gypsy. One of them, our girl Brittany, was getting a little senile as she aged. Her eyesight was failing as well. When we feed the dogs, they each have their own bowl and they all knew which one is theirs and never fought over them. We had one big bowl for Gypsy, and three smaller ones for the Dachshunds. One day we put their dinners out for them. Each dog was eating out of their own bowl when suddenly Brittany, all 7 pounds of her, stopped eating and wandered over to Gypsy's bowl and started to eat his food.  Gypsy, all 50 pounds of shepherd/husky mix, backed away from his bowl and looked at us with a "help me out here" look.

    Gypsy was always patient with the smaller dogs.  They would jump on him, lie on him, snuggle next to him, and rest their heads on his back.  He also used to have a rope toy that he would play with.  One of the other dogs would tug at the other end and Gypsy would gently hold one end in his mouth while the other dog, Disney, would yank and pull as hard as he could to try to get the rope toy away.  Gypsy would just sit with his paws crossed and watch, holding on but never growling or trying to pull the toy away.

## LOYALTY - PROTECTION

Dogs show their loyalty in many ways. They protect their owners and property. They protect you, sit by you follow, you around, follow your commands. Dogs are even loyal when we are not nice to them. Some people say that dogs that are abused remain loyal because they don't know any better. I guess you can say that about people who are in abusive relationships at home or at work too. It is hard to get out of those situations.

In most cases, loyalty is rewarded. Dogs get treats, and loving attention. People get promotions and respect. Loyalty doesn't guarantee your safety, especially if someone is manipulating you for his or her own advancement.

Susan Rogers talks about the loyalty one of her Airedales when a man started to bother her. Her dog took a bite out of him in an effort to protect her. It worked.

My dogs were always protective of me. When I was growing up our family dog, Tammy, felt it was her job to protect all of us kids. She was a collie, and Tammy used to herd us when were playing outside. She was always around, keeping a watchful eye on us.

Gypsy, my soul dog, followed me everywhere. He would jump on the couch and lean into me. He often did this if I was feeling down or sad.

Loyalty is a quality we look for in people when we seek to establish relationships, both personal and professional. It is hard to find that person who will always be loyal to you. Dogs will always be loyal. You are extremely fortunate if you get the loyalty from a person that you can rely on from a dog.

Dogs will protect their owners and what they consider to be their property or domain. My friend Kristen explains the protecting nature of dogs very well. "They pick up on our emotions, the way we react to other people. Rorie senses my tension. She stays right by me and is very protective. I remember one time I was dating someone and she would growl at him all the time. She would go ballistic if he went to my room. I think she had better judgment of a person's character than I did! They can sense the 'wrongness'; you can't fool them for long. As people, we tend to see what we want to see. Eventually, I had to choose between my boyfriend and Rorie. I chose Rorie."

Dogs are also very protective of their property. Anyone knocking on our front door, or ringing the doorbell will bring a running, barking, and sometimes growling dog. Anyone entering the yard, or passing by the house will cause barking, growling, perked up ears, hair raised on the back. Even the postal worker dropping off the mail in the mailbox brings this reaction.

Some dogs take their protection a little too far. Every year we exchange Christmas stockings to celebrate the holiday and we usually had stockings for the dogs as well. One Christmas, when we had Gypsy and Disney, we decided to give stockings to both of them. We had put a variety of dog treats in each stocking and had put them under the tree. Big mistake! Gypsy was indifferent. He sniffed his stocking but left it alone. Disney, on the other hand, would not leave his stocking. He pulled it further under the tree and sat next to it, not leaving it when we tried to coax him out. Every time Gypsy walked by the tree Disney would growl. Disney did not come out from under the tree, staying by his stocking all night. On Christmas morning we pulled the stocking out and opened some of the treats for Disney to eat. He was tired from staying up all night. We continued to have stockings for the dogs on Christmas but put them together that morning and did not leave them under the tree again!

Heidi Knowlton tells a wonderful story about the loyalty and protection of a foster dog, Pasha, a wolf hybrid she was caring for. " I was going outside with Pasha and had him on a leash. I also had an elderly St. Bernard, Clancy, on the other leash. We lived in the country with neighbors nearby who kept a rabbit in a hutch in their yard. Pasha had figured this out pretty quickly and was always looking over at the hutch. We were walking down a ramp and Clancy slipped, causing me to slip. I fell down and both leashes went flying out of my hands. Pasha took off and made a beeline for the hutch. He got about 30 yards away and suddenly stopped. He turned around and came back to us and sniffed us all over. I was still on the ground checking on Clancy and grabbed his leash. I guess it was more important for Pasha to make sure we were okay than to pursue that rabbit."

Disney

Disney protecting his stocking

## RESILIENCE

Sometimes we suffer in circumstances for a long time before we find our way out. Resilience is demonstrated in all of the following stories. When I was ten years old I kicked my brother in the 'nuts'. He was always pestering me in some way. On that day I discovered a way to protect myself from any man that was bothering me. He didn't bother me too much after that.

Two of my dogs, Gypsy and Petey, were rescues. Gypsy (my souldog) was abandoned and was on his own for a while before he found me.

One Saturday, on an unusually warm day in January, Gypsy got out of the apartment and took off. We immediately went looking for him, driving all over Milton for several hours calling his name and asking anyone if they had seen him. No luck in the search. Later in the day we called the Town Hall and Milton Dog Officer and left messages with Gypsy's tag number and our phone number. That night the temperature dropped rapidly into the single digits. Still no Gypsy. I barely slept, crying and with a huge lump in my throat as I worried for his safety and I thought we had lost him.

    The next morning we got a phone call from the Town Hall with information that someone had found Gypsy. He was wandering around her street and looked lost and this wonderful person kept Gypsy in her fenced in yard while she had to go off to work. She left a phone number and address. I looked at the address and saw that it was in Quincy, which was several miles away. I held out hope that he had somehow managed to travel that distance without getting hurt. After traveling 10 miles, we arrived at the house and I peaked through the fence. There was my Gypsy! I called his name and he looked at me with the most relieved expression. If he could have talked he would have said "You finally found me!". We got him into the car and drove home. For the next two days he slept, only getting up to go out and pee and to eat. I kept checking his breathing because he was so still, not moving at all for hours. He was exhausted and he walked funny because his paws were swollen from walking on the ice and snow. It wasn't the last time Gypsy took off on us but he never was lost again. He would take off but never far away and always circled back to the house. He had learned his lesson. I never had the opportunity to thank the person who found Gypsy but will be forever grateful for her caring and kindness in taking him in.

My sister Christine's dog, Cletis, had a similar experience. He escaped from the house one day and decided to go exploring. He soon became lost. Chris and her family looked for Cletis for days with no luck. Finally, they got a call that someone had picked up Cletis. Fortunately he was okay and has not disappeared since.

We can learn a lot about resilience from dogs. As dogs age they go blind, lose their hearing, slow down. Some can't walk either but they adapt. They find a way to adjust to their situation. And as owners, we learn to be patient. We develop empathy for others, both animal and human. Yes, dogs teach us great lessons about resilience in our treatment of others and in our acceptance of our own aging process.

I have a friend, Rita Schiano, who has a black Labrador named Jessie. While still in her early years, Jessie developed Progressive Retinal Atrophy, an eye disease that caused her to go completely blind. It is amazing how she has adapted to her home and surroundings, utilizing other senses, moving more slowly, and finding her way around.  Rita says, "Jessie can be fearless.  She still loves to play ball.  She uses her other senses to find it.  Her disability hasn't brought down her spirit.  She is still a very happy dog.  Her connectedness to us is what keeps her going.  She went through sadness and depression at the beginning.  Jessie has managed her emotions and pulled herself through."

    Even as Jessie became blind Rita would take her outside to play ball.  She threw a tennis ball that Jessie would chase.  Using her sense of hearing and smell, Jessie would find the ball and return it to Rita as she called her name.

Jessie

The most incredible story of resilience that I have heard is from my friends Sharon Johnson and Dorsie Kovacs and their dog Gus. On June 1, 2011 a tornado touched down near Springfield, Massachusetts. The F3 tornado's destructive path was a ½ mile wide and traveled 39 miles through cities and towns in

Western and Central Massachusetts. One of the towns that was hit very hard was the small town of Monson where Sharon Johnson and Dorsie Kovacs lived with their dog Gus, and a variety of other animals. Dorsie also worked in Monson as a veterinarian and was performing surgery on a dog when the storm came through. During the storm they lost power and heard that a tornado had passed close by. Dorsie finished up the surgery and left as soon as possible to get to her house.

When she got near her street she saw that all the trees were uprooted and knew that her house was badly damaged. To get to her house, Dorsie had to climb over, under, and around fallen trees and power lines. There was also a strong smell of gas permeating the air. She finally made it to the house and, despite the destruction, made her way inside, called out for Gus. She found Gus at the back door. He started wagging his tail. As Dorsie surveyed the house, she was amazed that Gus and one of her birds (a Cockatoo) had survived.

A couple of days after the tornado my spouse and I went over to Dorsie and Sharon's house to help with cleanup and offer any assistance they might need. Their home was destroyed. It was amazing to me that Gus had made it through this horrific storm. After the tornado experience, Gus did get scared in thunderstorms, shaking and most likely remembering that terrible day. Dorsie and Sharon lost their home but they rebuilt it and Gus was with them for a while longer in their new home before he passed away.

# Coming into Fullness of Life – Joy and Silliness

Frosty & K.G. Keough-Huff

## TELEPATHY – DOGNITION - VISUALIZATION

I have practiced visualization over the years in my athletic endeavors and in my career in coaching. I started learning about guided visualization in college when I was playing Lacrosse. As a goalie, I would practice visualizing making saves, with image after image of playing to perfection. This practice helped my confidence and I was able to have a great deal of success in goal, helping my team to compete, making it all the way to the national championship in 1979. Unfortunately we lost in the final, but it was close.

After college I wanted to stay in shape so I started running long distance. I ran in some 10K races and dreamed about running a marathon. After a few months I found a training program, joined a running club and decided to train for a marathon.

The program I was given was a 12-week program with the longest distance being an 18 mile run. At the time, I thought "how am I going to run 26.2 miles when the longest training run is 18 miles?" I mentioned it to my running coach and he said, "After mile 15, it's all mental." So, I signed up for a marathon and joined a workshop given by Dr. Steven Goldberg, author of <u>The Sports Mind.</u>

The workshop provided exercises in guided visualization and coping skills. I was able to take these exercises and apply them to my mental training for the marathon. It helped tremendously, as I finished the Hyannis marathon with a time that qualified me for Boston, which was my dream.

The Hyannis marathon took place in February, which is not the best time to run a marathon on Cape Cod. The marathon was a 2 loop course, with most of the runners signing up for the half marathon. I battled snow and freezing weather and utilized my mental cues and training to get me through the race, especially during the second loop, when I was running by myself most of the time. My ability to finish the race only solidified the belief I had in guided visualization and its use in obtaining goals.

I have coached a number of team sports over the years, using the power of positive thinking and guided visualization with some of my teams. Some of them didn't always buy into the concept but I did have some success with some teams. I remember coaching basketball at Milton Academy and I had a group of athletes that listened to, and seemed interested in, some of the exercises I did with them on positive thinking and guided visualization. So I had them do 'mental free throws' during practice as one of their regular drills. I kept track of our statistics that season and was amazed at the improvement in our free throw shooting. Most high schools free throw percentage is 50-60%. That year we shot 80% as a team.

I never really thought about visualization working with dogs but it makes sense. Every time I come home I can hear the dogs barking even before I have entered the driveway. Other times I am anticipating my spouse coming home and the dogs will begin going to the door and window to look out, several minutes before she arrives. Dogs have ESP (extra sensory perception)! Dogs are so close to their humans that they pick up on their emotions, feelings, thoughts, and illnesses. In fact, research is being done on dogs and their illnesses as they are diagnosed more often with "people" diseases, including diabetes, heart disease, and arthritis.

Sharon Johnson tells a story about Moses, a black lab/shepherd mix. "Moses was afraid of his own shadow. He always knew when he had to go to the vet. He would chew his nails off. He only did this the night prior to his appointment. This behavior only happened when he was going to the vet. It never happened any other time. I never said anything to him prior to the appointment. He just knew."

Dogs pick up on our energy and share it. They are emotionally connected to us. They pick up on our anxiety and stress as well as happiness and love. Dorsie Kovacs recalls how she came to get one of her favorite dogs, Gus. "A guy brought Gus in while I was meeting with a breeder about purchasing a Labrador retriever. I held him and he turned and kissed me. There was an instant connection. There was another buyer for Gus but the breeder recognized the connection and steered the buyer towards purchasing another dog. Gus was with us for many, many years."

Susan Rogers has observed and practiced telepathy a great deal with the dogs she has worked with over the years. She tells a story about a 10 month-old male Airedale she brought to a show. "He had not been trained. He had no experience and had not learned any commands. I brought him to get the experience. We went in the ring with 10 other dogs and he was first in line. The dog followed directions perfectly. The whole time I kept thinking about what he had to do, mentally running over in my mind each part of what he needed to do. It was amazing. I had never trained this dog and he did it just perfect. He came in first!"

Susan and I went on to discuss dogs and visualization. Susan uses a lot of visualization in her communication with dogs. "Spelling doesn't work. They know what you are thinking. You can channel and retrain a lot with a dog to change their behavior. Susan says "I don't know how my dog knows I am going on a trip when I don't have the suitcase out and there are no other clues that I am going anywhere. They always seem to know when I am leaving though."

In working with and caring for her dogs, Susan has used visualization to reduce anxiety and lessen her dog's stress. She visualizes what she is going to do, where she is going, and if the dog is coming with her, how they should behave. Her dogs are calmer and well behaved when traveling in a car because of the practice of visualization. Susan believes it is a good tool to use for people who are able to project their thoughts. Dogs are more perceptive that we realize.

### FUNNY STUFF & EEWW GROSS!

The reason a dog has so many friends is that he wags his tail instead of his tongue.
– Anonymous

Dorsie Kovacs shared several stories from her career as a veterinarian and as an owner of many dogs and other animals. She remembers a time when they had a puppy and a neighbor had walked by her house with her child. The dog proceeded to show his affection by licking the child's face, covering it with kisses. All of a sudden the mother came running over, grabbed her child and put him under her arm. She ran over to a garden hose and started spraying her son, hosing him down to get the 'puppy germs' off. Her son was screaming. The woman started yelling at Dorsie, saying "I am a nurse and they have germs!" Talk about overreacting!

Sharon Johnson and Dorsie at one time had 2 dogs, Gus and Roxanne. Sharon tells this story as one that fits into the "Ewww…Gross category. "Roxanne was ill. She had terrible diarrhea and had gone all over the dining room. Gus, our golden retriever, thought it was great. He decided to roll in it and then shake his fur. I came home and the smell was overpowering, and the diarrhea was everywhere! On the walls, floor, and furniture. It took a long time to clean up the dogs and the dining room smelled pretty nasty."

Dorsie recalls a client coming into the clinic with one dog on 2 leashes! "He was a little 6-7 pound Chihauwa that constantly attacked his owners ankles, trying to bite them. So he had the 2 leashes to pull him away from one ankle, and the other to pull away from the other. It was hilarious. "The dog was a real challenge but he still loved him."

Rita Schiano's dog Frisco was a shepherd mix. One time Rita took Frisco to a dog show and registered Frisco as a "Venetian Shepherd". The person taking her information stated that she had never heard of that breed. Rita stuck by her assertion of the breed and I believe Frisco is the only Venetian shepherd that ever existed!

My friends Pam and Pat Patterson had a dog named Doc. He was a huge blue tick coonhound. We would stop by to visit and he would come bounding into the kitchen and slobber all over us. I adored him and so did they. However, I would have drool all over me when I left. Pam and Pat saved many dogs over the years. Dogs that were given up, abused, or abandoned. Their house was chaotic but full of love. Pat used to tell me story after story about their dogs. His eyes would just light up when he talked about Bailey, Snickers, Bubba, Angel, and Doc.

    I guess this next story is called 'Disney and the Tampons'. One day I noticed that our small trash container in our bathroom was tipped over. I saw there were used tampons in the container. It looked like one of our dogs had gotten into the garbage. So I waited, and sure enough, the next day when I let the dogs out to "do their business", I watched Disney poop out a long one with a tail! He had eaten one of the tampons! Eeeww! Gross!!

## SPONTANIETY - CURIOSITY

I think that when dogs and people do things spontaneously it can be funny, exhilarating, dangerous, and can sometimes get you in trouble! The most memorable instance of spontaneity was one that I shared with one of my angels, Petey. When I tell the story to others, I call it "Petey jumps off the cliff."

This death-defying story happened the day Petey jumped off an embankment that had at least a 10 foot drop. We were on vacation, staying with family at a cottage on Lake Erie in Pennsylvania. It was a beautiful place, right on the water. There was a grassy area of about 75 yards that led to stairs going down to the beach. It was a nice, warm day in July and we had been there a couple of days when I decided to bring Petey down to the beach. I had to carry him down the stairs as they were very steep and too difficult for a miniature dachshund to descend.

As soon as I go to the bottom of the stairs, I put Petey down and he started to wander around. I kept an eye on him and followed wherever he went. Within a couple of minutes he had found a dead, decaying fish.

I picked him up before he could touch it and walked away from it. I put him down and he immediately turned and headed straight back toward the fish! I realized that Petey could not stay at the beach so I picked him up and headed up the stairs.

I got to the top of the stairs and walked to the beginning of the grassy area (about 20 feet) and put Petey down on the ground, facing the cottage. Unfortunately he immediately turned around and headed full-speed towards the embankment. He went off the edge and dropped at least 10 feet down into very thick brush. I ran to the edge of the embankment yelling his name. "Petey! Petey!" Louder and louder I called. I couldn't see or hear him at all so I ran down the stairs going to the beach and jumped into the brush. I started lifting branches and logs trying to find him. I was in an absolute panic! At the same time my nephew Mark, my sister Pam, and my brother-in-law Ray, had heard me yelling and had come running from the beach.

I finally saw 2 little eyes peeking at me through some branches. Petey was completely trapped. I broke branches, lifting huge tree logs, climbed into and over downed trees to get to him. I reached Petey, grabbed and held him to me. He was in a panic but not crying. I then realized that I was now trapped in the brush too! My brother-in-law was reaching over the railing of the stairs to help me. I went to pass Petey to him but Petey then screamed and cried out so I held him against my body and he quieted down. I ended up butt sliding along a log, reaching my free hand out to my brother-in-law who helped me climb out. I finally got free and climbed up the stairs with Petey wrapped in a towel, and started heading towards the cottage.

    In the meantime my nephew had run to the cottage to alert everyone else that something had happened to Petey. As I walked with Petey in my arms, wrapped in the towel, I looked up and saw that everyone (we had family and visitors) was on the deck looking down with worried looks on their faces. I had no idea if Petey was hurt so I put him on the grass to see if he could walk. He started running towards the cottage as if nothing had happened. He was fine! I made it to the deck and someone said to me "Are you alright?" I looked down at my legs and clothes and noticed I had cuts, mud, and blood all over me. My heart was still racing and I was a mess! My nephew came up to me and gave me a big hug and said, "that was the bravest thing I have ever seen."

I went and showered and finally calmed down but I had cuts and bruises and was sore for a couple of days. The next day I went to the beach and tried to lift one of the logs that I had moved to get to Petey. I couldn't move it at all. I don't know where I summoned the strength to move the logs to get to Petey but it is amazing what we will do for our animals.

When talking with my niece Samantha about spontaneity, she described a time when she was driving her car and had one of their dogs, Maggie, in the back seat. Samantha had the window opened a little so that Maggie could get air but kept it mostly up because she was worried that Maggie might try to jump out the window. All of a sudden she heard a click. Looking back to check on Maggie, she noticed that she had put her paw on the window button and the window had rolled all the way down. Maggie had stuck her head out the window!

When Gypsy had only been with us a few weeks, we tried gating him in the kitchen while we went out. As he saw us heading to the door, he tried to leap over the gate. He didn't make it. Sometimes we can learn a lesson from the results of a spontaneous action. Gypsy never tried to jump the gate again.

Gypsy was always spontaneously running off. Any time he had saw an open door he liked to escape. He never really went far away after the incident where he got lost and ended up 10 miles away. As he got older he would get out and just run up and down the street. We would sit on the front steps and call for him. Gypsy would just run by and look at us with this huge smile on his face. Then we would get the car and drive up next to him and Gypsy would jump right in, happy as could be!

Susan Rogers recalled several humorous stories where one of her Airedales did something she never anticipated happening. This particular dog was a prankster. She had managed to open her cage and let herself out. She then proceeded to let all the females out of their cages where they went and peed in all the male dog's water buckets! Another time Susan remembers the same Airedale running around with a bra in her mouth and bringing books out into the room to chew on.

My friend Diane Mossa described a day when she was driving with her dog, Bailey, in the car. She stopped at a car repair shop and Bailey immediately jumped out of the car and took off, running down Rt. 9, a very busy road. "I chased him down Rt. 9, running as fast as I could. Thankfully, he stopped in someone's yard to sniff another dog. I ran along the fence that enclosed most of the yard and crept up behind and grabbed him. I never would have caught him if he hadn't stopped. " Yes, spontaneity can get you in trouble!

My friends Dorsie Kovacs and Sharon Johnson had a Terrier named Roxanne. She was a small dog with a big attitude. She interacted with their other dogs, Critter and Crackers, but could care less about Dorsie and Sharon. "Roxanne was a 'superstar' dog. She would parade down Commercial Street in Provincetown when we would go to visit friends there. She would run off and jump in the water, then come back to us." "We had a glass coffee table and Roxanne would always go underneath it to try to get to whatever was resting on the table from under the table. It was so funny."

Roxanne would follow anyone. Sharon describes one time that they were at their lakefront cottage in Otis, Massachusetts. Roxanne would see someone go by in a boat or kayak and she would dive off the dock, taking off after them. She would swim across the lake and be gone for hours. We expected that one day she would not return but she always came back."

      Sometimes people do spontaneous things. It can be exhilarating and fun. You can also get into trouble. Whenever I get the urge to do something spontaneous, I always take a breath and think about Petey's 10 foot drop and my spectacular save. Sometimes I go for it and other times I just smile and think "no way, not today". I think some dog's share that thought process, especially as they get older.

# Aging and Saying Goodbye

**Nicky & Petey**

## DOGGY DEMENTIA

We can learn a lot from dogs about the aging process. Dogs get dementia just like people, with similar symptoms and behaviors. People get forgetful. Dogs do too! Driving somewhere in the car and then forgetting where you are going, not being able to find the words and angry outbursts are symptoms of people dementia.

Two of my dogs, Brittany and Petey, demonstrated signs of Doggie Dementia as they aged. Brittany would wake up at all hours during the night and start barking. She had a loud piercing bark and would go on and on. She never did this until she got old. During the day we often found her facing a wall, just staring at it and wagging her tail. She wasn't sure where she was. Blindness also became an issue for her as well.

Petey has recently shown signs of dementia. He sometimes forgets where he is and has accidents. The anxiety that plagued him as a puppy has returned and gotten much worse as his eyesight has declined. Where we once had 4 dogs, we are left with just Petey. I think he misses his buddies. He seems much more fearful. He definitely suffers from abandonment syndrome. He hates it when we have to leave.

Susan Rogers boarded a dog at her kennel that was extremely nervous. Over time she got less nervous but would engage in a curious pattern of behavior, barking 3 times then stopping, barking 3 times again, all the time looking at the wall, which could have definitely been a sign of dementia.

I remember when my mother was in her final days. She was in a rehabilitation center before she was brought home for hospice care. Her health had declined rapidly and her condition was terminal. While visiting her at the rehabilitation center, I noticed her moving her left hand along the sheet in a stroking motion. I asked her what she was doing. She looked at me and smiled and said "I am patting the dog, silly." I always felt that the dogs that were in her life (Tammy and Frosty especially) and who have passed on are with her now.

Dogs are now used for therapy in long-term care facilities. Their presence helps people maintain a positive attitude. Therapy dogs help older people by bringing joy into their life, providing companionship, a sense of connection through touch and communication, helping to cope with illness and loss, and stimulating exercise and activity. Now that I have a dog with signs of dementia, I am reversing our roles. I am trying to provide to my dog what therapy dogs provide to older people. I give him a lot more attention, trying to anticipate his needs to reduce his anxiety and stress. I try to nurture him they way my dogs taught me over the years. Hopefully, I have learned the lessons they provided through the many times they took care of me.

## DIGNITY

Susan Rodgers has spent a lifetime as a dog trainer, breeder, kennel owner, and has shown her Airedales all around the country. Susan's Airedales have won numerous awards throughout her career. Susan says "Airedales show tremendous dignity. They never want to get caught doing anything wrong. Instead they pull pranks in private. In public, they have a dignified air, looking off into the distance, head turned aside looking over their shoulder."

Tammy, our family dog while I was growing up, always sat with her nose up, gazing over her yard. She was always watching over us. As she aged and began to have 'accident's, she would drop her head and look so ashamed. We understood that she couldn't help it and it was painful to see the look of embarrassment in her eyes. Tammy was never reprimanded for her accidents, but it was clear that she recognized what was happening.

My dog Gypsy, the shepherd/husky mix demonstrated a dignified manner as he aged. He was so good and patient with the 3 miniature dachshunds we had. He would often lie down somewhere and one or all of the dachshunds would end up lying on or around him.

    I admire people who age with dignity. My father was a quiet, unassuming man who always carried himself with dignity. It showed in the decisions he made. He had a doctorate in chemistry from MIT and while he was working for a corporation in the early 60's, he was contacted by a government agency to develop a chemical weapon to be used by the military. He refused. My father may have lost the opportunity for a secure income but he kept his dignity and always valued his 'moral compass'. As he aged, he continued to live independently, struggling with dementia and other health issues. He was always fearful of not being able to take care of himself. When it finally happened and he was in a rehabilitation facility, his dementia became worse but in some ways it was a blessing. The things that he worried about didn't seem to matter anymore and he seemed at peace.

## HAVING ACCIDENTS

Dogs have accidents. Some dogs have this issue throughout their lives. Most dogs are house trained but as they age, accidents begin to occur for some, just like people! Petey, our anxious and fearful dog, began to exhibit signs of dementia and frequently began to have accidents. Getting a "doggie diaper" for him proved challenging. The small diaper was too small and the medium diaper was too big. He would just walk out of it. We ended up using a maxi pad with an ace bandage wrapped around him to hold it on. Everyone who saw him thought he was injured and would ask if he was okay. We would explain the situation and they would laugh or often say "oh, that's so sad."

Cleaning up and constantly checking areas of the house when Petey decides to wander has been a challenge as pee is hard to see on a wood floor. Easy to clean up once you find it (or step in it). Leaving him in a crate was not an option, as he thought nothing of peeing on himself or pooping and then sitting in it. So I have developed a patience and understanding for this behavior. He can't help it. And I know someday I may have the same issues. Once again I am learning from dogs.

## SAYING GOODBYE

During the writing of this book, I have laughed and cried over many of the stories I recalled of my experiences with my own dogs. As I interviewed people for the book, including friends who had dogs, professionals who worked with dogs, the same emotions emerged as they told their stories. Tears were shed, laughter so hard it made some cry. There were great stories and wonderful remembrances. I had several people thank me for helping them remember experiences with their dogs that they hadn't thought about in awhile or had forgotten. Every person I interviewed cried and laughed as they told their stories. It was very emotional for the interviewer and interviewee. I had such a wonderful time with the process of interviewing and writing up their recollections, that I almost lost my focus in bringing the book to completion.

This chapter I saved until the end. I knew this would be the most difficult to write as it was for those who contributed their thoughts on saying goodbye to their four pawed angels.

Susan Rodgers talks about her dog Gillis, whom she felt knew she was leaving this world. "I brought her to Dorsie and she asked, "When did Gillis go blind?" Susan says, "Her eyes were all white, she walked around and then held her paw out and got the injection. She went so quickly."

Diane Mossa talks about Bailey, her first dog that she had adopted. "Bailey was neglected and I was not as patient with him. I wish I had known more about him but he was my first dog. It was the hardest thing I ever did. I had to make the choice. He wasn't eating and he was 15 years old. I took him to the Sturbridge animal care where there was a very nice funeral area. My friends took me and after the burial we cried for hours." Diane continues with tears springing to her eyes. "I waited a few months. I was heartbroken. A friend came over and said she knew someone who had to give up 2 Shih Tzu's and was wondering if I would take them. The minute I saw Bandit and Zeus I wanted them. They were well taken care of. In the beginning they thought they were just visiting. It took awhile for them to acclimate. Bandit had allergies and had to be put on Prednizone. They also had mites, which took a while to get rid of. I will never forget Bailey but Bandit and Zeus have been wonderful for me. I adore them."

Dorsie Kovacs and Sharon Johnson shared their saying goodbye stories through tears of sadness and joy in remembrance of their pets who have moved on. Dorsie, in her career as a veterinarian has been at the end of a dog's life so many times. "After putting dogs down I have had several people tell me they have seen the dog in the house, that their spirit is still there. So I will tell people not to be surprised if this happens." Dorsie says.

Sharon shares a remembrance of their Golden Retriever named Critter. "She was a smart dog. We put her to sleep at home and buried her ashes in our yard. We decided to have a celebration and talk about her life. We got a bottle of champagne and popped the cork. Critter used to love to chase the corks when we opened a bottle. Well, the cork flew in the air and landed right on her grave. At the same time a beam of sunlight broke through the clouds, shining right on the grave. You couldn't have scripted it any better. We laughed and cried and knew that Critter was still with us. Our other golden retriever, Crackers, missed Critter for quite a long time. One time we were at our vacation home in Otis and Crackers saw another golden, ran up to it thinking it was Critter, realized it wasn't and walked away."

    I remembered the same thing happened when my Gypsy first met Petey. Petey looked a lot like Disney, and Gysy and Disney were inseparable for 9 years. We brought Petey into the house and Gypsy ran up to him wagging his tail. He sniffed Petey, his tail stopped wagging, his head dropped, and he sadly walked away. However, spending several years together, Gypsy and Petey became great friends.

    Saying goodbye is so painful and difficult. Whether it is your person or dog friend, it can be devastating. There are some people who say that you can't possibly have the same heartbreak and grief for a dog as you do for a person. I disagree. I have never had to make the decision to end a person's life like I have with a dog. I have taken care of, supported, and prayed over family and friends who have either been in hospice or in a nursing home for their final days. And I have held hands and paws as they have passed on. The grief and sadness was there each time. I remember holding my mothers hand and saying the Lord's Prayer as she passed. She had been given a terminal diagnosis of pulmonary fibrosis and had made the decision to spend her final days at home. Having all her family around was important and I know it helped her to know we were all there. It was the same with my father. My experiences with my dogs have been similar. As painful as it was, I wanted to be with them in the end, so they would not be alone.

      Disney started getting sick when he was around 6 years old. He would get pneumonia and was on antibiotics constantly. He finally passed away at the age of 9. It was our first loss and it was heartbreaking. We had been going to Tufts Animal hospital in Grafton, Massachusetts for his care, and in spite of all the tremendous care and efforts to save him, his heart finally gave out. We cried for days and our other dog, Gypsy, became depressed.

      Brittany was spunky until the end. She couldn't see, had dementia, waking up at all hours, barking at the wall. She was aging gracefully until she stopped eating, going days without trying to eat anything offered. The decision to have her put down was so difficult. We were on vacation in Pennsylvania, and the decision had to be made. Brittany was so uncomfortable and nothing was working to help her. We couldn't get pain medication or anything into her system. I always felt like there might have been something else we could have done to save her. But there wasn't. It was her time. Brittany lived to the age of 17.

And then it was time to say goodbye to my Soul Dog, Gypsy. We had moved to our new house with Gypsy, Nicky, and Petey. Gypsy was really getting thin. He didn't eat much, and when he did it went right through him. We spoke with our veterinarian, Dorsie Kovacs, who agreed to come to the house, as we all knew it was time. Gypsy was my buddy and tears are flowing even now as I remembered him that day over 6 years ago. I probably waited too long, as he suffered with his painful hips and constant diarrhea but I didn't want him to go. He passed on so peacefully as I held him in my arms. Gypsy also lived to the age of 17.

Nicky, my little man, had cancer. It was on his face and near his eye and mouth. He became increasingly uncomfortable as the tumors grew. It became difficult for him to eat, although Pumpkin Pie filling and anything I was eating seemed to interest him. I would chew up whatever I was eating, like a mama bird feeding her young. Despite medication, Nicky's pain became too much and he stopped eating. We knew it was time. I was in tears because he was suffering and I didn't want to let him go. But we had to. His suffering ended quickly with us holding him and petting him with Dorsie taking care of the euthanasia. Nicky also lived to the age of 17.

 I will always remember Nicky and my dear friend Lydia Walz, who passed away from cancer in 2009. Nicky was not very friendly with people and Lydia liked cats and really wasn't a dog lover. We had sold our house and needed a place to stay for a week while we waited to move in to our new place. Lydia and her partner Lizi Brown, gave us the use of their studio to stay in for the week.

 At the time we knew that Lydia wasn't feeling well but had no idea she had cancer. She didn't know yet either. I think Nicky knew though. He would walk up to Lydia who was sitting in a chair and sit with her. I remember them sitting that way for a couple of hours one night. We joked, "Look at Nicky sitting with Lydia the cat lover." A week after we moved into our new home we found out that Lydia had been to the doctor and been diagnosed with Stage 4 Esophageal cancer. Six weeks later she passed away.

When is the right time to say goodbye? Most veterinarians will so "You'll know when its time." But it is so difficult when the time actually comes to say goodbye. During the editing of this book my last angel, Petey, passed away. Once again I experienced the heartbreak of losing my buddy who had been with me for many years.

We knew Petey was not well. He had been diagnosed with a liver condition which even though medication was helping, his age and the progression of the mass on his liver caused his health to deteriorate rapidly. Petey loved to eat food. His food, my food, anything. We always thought that when he stopped eating, that would be the signal that it was time to let him go. And that's what happened. He stopped eating. And then stopped drinking water. We knew it was time and yet it was so painful to say our last goodbye.

I miss him so much. The hardest part is when I come home to an empty house. No barking, no wagging tail, no begging for food. I know that he had a good life with us and because of him I know that I will rescue more dogs. I will need time to grieve but the time will come when a dog will rescue me once again.

Lydia Walz & Nicky

## Rainbow Bridge
-Author unknown

Just this side of heaven is a place called Rainbow Bridge.
When an animal dies that has been especially close to someone here, that pet goes to Rainbow Bridge.
There are meadows and hills for all of our special friends so they can run and play together. There is plenty of food, water and sunshine, and our friends are warm and comfortable.
All the animals who had been ill and old are restored to health and vigor. Those who were hurt or maimed are made whole and strong again. Just as we remember them in our dreams of days and times gone by.
The animals are happy and content, except for one small thing; they each miss someone very special to them, who had to be left behind.
They all run and play together, but the day comes when one suddenly stops and looks into the distance. His bright eyes are intent. His eager body quivers.
Suddenly he begins to run from the group, flying over the green grass, his legs carrying him faster and faster.
You have been spotted, and when you and your special friend finally meet, you cling together in joyous reunion, never to be parted again.

The happy kisses rain upon your face; your hands again caress the beloved head, and you look once more into the trusting eyes of your pet, so long gone from your life but never absent from your heart.

Then you cross Rainbow Bridge together......

## DREAMS

When I was a goalie in lacrosse I would go to sleep at night and wake up with the sheets all tangled and wrapped around me. I was making saves in my sleep! Some people talk in their sleep. Dogs dream too! They talk in their sleep, run in their sleep. Gypsy, Brittany and Nicky all used to bark quietly and run in their sleep. Their paws would be moving as if they were chasing something and they seemed to be smiling.

I think Petey had dreams as well. He would wake suddenly in the middle of the night and cry a little bit, then move as close to me as possible before going back to sleep. He was either trying to get warm or wanted comfort and protection.

I have a dream about Rainbow Bridge. I am on the other side ready to cross over. I look and see my mother and father with Tammy sitting in between them. Frosty is sitting in front of my mother. Then I see them. My Angels! Disney, Gypsy, Nicodemus, Brittany, and Petey. They are all looking at me, tails wagging. They can see me!

There is a saying that sometimes when a door closes, a window opens. I'd like to add to this phrase by noting that sometimes the door shuts and you may feel you are in a room with no windows. If this happens, you must create a window. And sometimes you need help opening that window. Don't be afraid. Don't be afraid to ask for help. We all need help at some point in our lives. So open that window of opportunity and step into the next chapter of your life.

Recognize when you are needed. Help others, people and animals, whose doors may be shut, where they may be trapped. Help them open their window where hope lives and dreams can come true. That is my dream.

Dog – John Grabosky

## Acknowledgements

This book was a joy to write. It took a long time to finish as I enjoyed the process of interviewing and hearing so many stories a little too much. I kept looking to find one more interview, or one more story. I finally had to stop!

Thank you from the bottom of my heart to all of the people and animals who contributed to Four Pawed Angels.

A huge thank you to the Monson Small Animal Clinic for the many years of tremendous care they provided to our dogs.

Special thanks to Pam Doucette for her comments, suggestions, and editing of this book.

Front Cover – Gypsy & Disney at Milton Academy 1994
Back Cover – Petey 2015

**Dedication**

To Pat Patterson and John Grabosky, both passed away before the completion of this book. These wonderful men encouraged the writing of Four Pawed Angels. Neither knew each other. They each had the same twinkle in their eyes as they recalled the stories of their dog angels and how they enriched their lives.

To my wife Chris who has experienced with me the joys of dogs owning us.

## Recommended Websites & Readings

Abby's Little Friends Dog Rescue
      To make donations: Abby's Little Friends Dog Rescue 3713 Springwood Dr. Naples, FL  34104  Visit the website at abby'slittlefriends.com

Davis, Kathy <u>Therapy Dogs </u>(Howell Book House)

Kluger, Jeffrey  "Dog Interrupted"  Time Magazine Vol. 185, No. 8 2015 pp 40-43,

Schiano, Rita  <u>Live A Flourishing Life </u>The Reed Edwards Company, Copyright 2011

Ziegler, Katie E.  "The Human-Dog Bond"  2012 Therapy Dogs of Vermont

<u>http://www.therapydogs.org</u>
<u>http://www.dog-play.com</u>

# About The Author

Karen Keough-Huff starting writing and self-publishing books upon retiring after more than 30 years in education. Karen has published 2 other books, <u>The Viking and The Mayflower</u>, and <u>Sarah's Hope</u>. She resides in Massachusetts with her wife Chris and the memories of their four-pawed angels.